Zero Trust and Third-Party Risk

Reduce the Blast Radius

Gregory C. Rasner

To my wife, Maria, who has been amazingly supportive as I've worked on this book. You are always loved.

Contents

Foreword

Zero trust is like kung fu.

Before we get into a debate about whether Brazilian jiu jitsu or Krav Maga is better, I'm just using kung fu as a general term for the personal discipline involved in mastering a martial art. Zero trust is the discipline of protecting yourself and your community in the cyber world.

In the cyber world, it's illegal to attack back, so our discipline is defensive.

Our adversaries don't have the element of surprise anymore. We know what they're after: money, information, secrets. We also know how they get it. No matter what technology you use, what industry you're in, or what role you may play in your organization, the one common denominator of the thing that attackers exploit is trust. We've evolved our defense to focus on trust relationships in digital systems, hence the name *zero trust*.

Our discipline focuses on how to remove the trust relationships in digital systems. In my book, *Project Zero Trust* (Ascent Audio, 2022), I argue that everyone inside your organization should play a role in your zero trust effort, both inside IT and outside of IT.

But what about people outside of your company? Your partners, your suppliers, your vendors?

Most martial arts can be traced back to a school or group of people who founded it as a school of thought. For zero trust, John Kindervag is the kung fu master.

In 2010, while he was the lead analyst for cybersecurity at Forrester Research, John coined the term *zero trust*. In these two words, John attempted to distill the most successful strategy for preventing breaches that he had seen deployed in real companies around the world.

John wrote this strategy, not just for security people who were already starting to make a shift in their defensive strategies based on changes to technology and our adversaries' evolving tactics but for everyone else in information technology as well. Zero trust isn't just for us security nerds. We need everyone in our organizations to help.

In *Project Zero Trust*, I worked with John to create a fictional case study about a company that uses his repeatable five-step design methodology and his zero trust maturity model to secure their systems after a ransomware incident. I brought my experiences as a chief information security officer to highlight how organizations can apply zero trust to every critical aspect of cybersecurity: from physical security to enterprise resource planning (ERP) or customer relationship management (CRM) software, to identity, to cloud, DevOps, and security operations centers.

In other words, I wrote my book for your internal team.

But even if you get everything right in your own organization, that might not be enough in your zero trust journey. Today, two-thirds of all breaches are caused by vendors. Even if you've gotten everything right in your organization, you may have a blind spot to one of your biggest risks.

If zero trust is like kung fu, then Gregory Rasner is one of the blackbelts.

Gregory Rasner literally wrote the book on cybersecurity and third-party risk. And now he's applied zero trust to third-party risk to help complete our defense. We are stronger together than we are apart, and ensuring that your vendors or partners are secure is critical to success when it comes to cybersecurity.

Right now, when you think of third-party risk and zero trust, I hope you're picturing one of those kung fu movies where the heroes have to fight side by side, sometimes intertwined, doing incredibly intricate and daring moves to thwart their adversaries. That's a pretty good analogy for how you'll be able to work with your partners to defend yourselves together after reading Gregory Rasner's book.

—George Finney
CEO, Well Aware Security and author of *Project Zero Trust*

INTRODUCTION: Reduce the Blast Radius

A breach of your third and fourth parties is mathematically inevitable. The Identity Theft Resource Center reported a 14 percent increase in data breaches in 2022 over the preceding year, which follows a 68 percent increase from 2020 to 2021 (and 2020 broke the 2017 record with a 23 percent increase). The concept of zero trust operates on the assumption that a breach will happen, and it produces a strategy designed to reduce the impact (the *blast radius*) of that inevitable breach or incident. Considering the continued exponential growth of malicious cyber activities and the fact that most organizations have numerous vendors, embracing a zero trust strategy becomes the most reliable way to significantly decrease your vulnerability to third-party cyber risks.

In the past several years, cybersecurity risk in third-party risk management has increased significantly as malicious and criminal cybersecurity activity has also increased (up 800 percent since early 2020 according to FBI cyber reporting). In late 2021, the SolarWinds breach occurred, where a highly skilled and persistent actor utilized widely used software to infiltrate its ultimate targets: large technology companies and many three-letter governmental agencies. This breach served as a wake-up call for the cybersecurity and third-party risk management communities—a tangible example of a very dangerous and capable hacking organization leveraging a vendor to gain access to their intended targets/victims. Since then, the frequency of potential and actual breaches involving third and even higher-level parties has risen substantially, impacting organizations in a similar manner to the escalation in cyber activities. Even before 2020, organizations were struggling with the challenges of cyber and third-party risk management. And then, the exponential increase in cyber incidents, breaches, and related events within their vendor networks has posed additional difficulties, even for companies with mature risk management programs. Considering all of this, how can we reduce the risks in this space when cyber activity is growing exponentially and advanced persistent threat actors are taking advantage of control gaps?

Recently, a new strategy has been gaining headway: zero trust. Zero trust operates on the premise that a breach is inevitable, and its objective is to reduce the impact caused by such breaches. There is some truth to the idea that breaches are inevitable or bound to happen, considering the increasing number of cybersecurity and technology companies that have experienced breaches, despite having strong cybersecurity measures in place. This mindset also aligns with the reality that risk is never zero or completely eliminated. Cyber teams work to reduce risk; they cannot eliminate it entirely. Zero trust means implementing measures to protect assets and adopting a more mature identity and access management process, which will include incorporating features, such as multifactor authentication, least privilege, and enhanced network access controls.

Considering that the level of malicious cyber activity is unlikely to decrease anytime soon, if ever, it's unrealistic to expect a reduction in the number of cyber incidents, events, and breaches.

Does anyone think that the lesson that the advanced persistent actors took from the SolarWinds breach was to stop doing the same in the future? SolarWinds showed how easy it is for a malicious actor to use a third party to get access when customers don't hold their vendors to a cyber security standard. From the viewpoint of zero trust, a breach is inevitable, especially at your third parties. Therefore, adopting the strategy of zero trust becomes crucial to minimize the blast radius when a third-party breach occurs. Implementing a zero trust approach to third-party risk and vendors allows for a far greater reduction of risk because it requires an organization to compartmentalize and cordon off areas with segmentation and access controls. Zero trust can be a challenge to implement in many organizations as they struggle to determine where to start their strategy. Starting the journey with cyber third-party risk management provides an area to deploy that is easily defined, and this can often lead to enhanced risk reduction compared to other areas within a company.

The book is structured into two main parts: Part I provides an overview of the intersection between zero trust and third-party risk management, and then discusses the implementation of each domain: users, devices, and applications. Because zero trust is not a technology or a product, the emphasis is on processes, programs, and controls. Part I provides detailed insights into the necessary processes, programs, and controls for implementing zero trust in cyber third-party risk management, incorporating relevant examples and use cases whenever possible. Part II centers around the experiences of a fictitious company called KC Enterprises, which was introduced originally in my previous book, *Cybersecurity and Third-Party Risk: Third Party Threat Hunting* (Wiley, 2021). KC Enterprises suffers a breach caused by a third party, prompting them to begin their journey of zero trust and third-party risk management. Part II also allows you to observe how an organization implements a zero trust strategy to effectively mitigate vendor-related risks. It builds upon the lessons from Part I, offering practical insights into reducing vendor risk via the implementation of zero trust principles.

PART

I

Zero Trust and Third-Party Risk Explained

1

Overview of Zero Trust and Third-Party Risk

The intersection of zero trust (ZT) and third-party risk (TPR) can be a challenging one to cross. Neither is a set of technologies. Instead, both are a combination of people, processes, and technologies to accomplish a strategy. Implementing them isn't as simple as buying and installing a bunch of new stuff and walking away; it requires a way to find the overlap between the two (ZT and TPR) and making informed decisions to identify the changes required and carrying them out.

Zero Trust

Zero trust can be intimidating for any organization to implement, given that it is not a technology but changes to how specific security controls are accomplished in the enterprise. The next pages briefly cover the history of ZT to enable you to better understand the principles and then see the overlap with TPR.

What Is Zero Trust?

Zero trust is a strategy—it is not a tool or technology. To better understand the strategy, it is necessary to understand who developed it, why, and how. ZT was borne out of John Kindervag's observation that the previous trust model (perimeter-based security) was the fundamental cause of most data breaches. Kindervag expanded on this concept in "No More Chewy Centers: Introducing the Zero Trust Model of Information Security"[1]. In 2016, John updated his research with "No More Chewy Centers: The Zero Trust Model for Information Security, Vision: The Security Architecture and Operations Playbook."[2] The term *chewy center* derives from the previous (old) model in which information security professionals wanted their network to be like M&Ms: hard on the outside but with a soft and chewy center.

The perimeter-based, firewall-focused security models were ineffective against threats. The assumption that we trust all users, applications, and transactions once they've passed the firewall is folly and has been proven time and again to be wrong. Which interface is trusted and which untrusted? How do we know which packets to trust? Many attacks come from malicious insiders who are already inside the chewy center, munching away at the lack of controls past the crunchy outside.

ZT does not seek to gain trust but assumes all traffic is untrusted. The requirement in ZT becomes to ensure that

[1]John Kindervag, *No More Chewy Centers: Introducing the Zero Trust Model of Information Security*, September 14, 2010, Updated September 17, 2010, `https://media.paloaltonetworks.com/documents/Forrester-No-More-Chewy-Centers.pdf`
[2]John Kindervag, "No More Chewy Centers: The Zero Trust Model of Information Security, Vision: The Security Architecture and Operations Playbook", March 23, 2016, `https://crystaltechnologies.com/wp-content/uploads/2017/12/forrester-zero-trust-model-information-security.pdf`

resources are accessed securely, wherever they are located, require least privilege for access, strictly enforce access controls, and all traffic is logged and inspected. This approach eliminates the chewy center by removing trust from the process.

The Importance of Strategy

Zero trust is not a project but an updated approach to thinking about information security. As previously mentioned, ZT is a strategy, not a tool or technology. Strategy is defined as "a plan of action or policy designed to achieve a major or overall aim." A successful strategy requires structure, and one of the most widely used comprises the four levels of warfare: policy, strategy, tactics, and operations. Policy has the overall grand strategy or political outcome as the ultimate goal—for example, the grand strategy in World War II for the Allies was the unconditional surrender of the Axis powers. Under the policy is the strategy. Using the same WWII analogy, this would be the European and Asia Theater strategies for conquering the Axis powers in those regions. Tactics are the things used and include the tools of war (tanks, planes, ships, etc.), and operations are the way the tools are used (battles, engagements, etc.).

Taking that same outlook on cyber strategy, the grand strategy is to stop all data breaches. That should be borne out through all downstream activities as the outcome of this grand strategy. The strategy at the next level is ZT. To successfully meet the top-level grand strategy, ZT will be the "big idea" deployed down into the tactics and operations. Tactics are the tools and technologies leveraged to achieve the ZT strategy, and operations are the policies and governance that ensure successful execution up the strategy stack.

Connecting the strategy and ultimate goals of ZT drives the definition: a strategy designed to stop data breaches and make other cyberattacks unsuccessful by eliminating trust from digital systems.

Concepts of Zero Trust

Three concepts are crucial to the success of any ZT strategy: secure all resources, strictly enforce access controls, and verify always. These concepts derive from the strategy that you can no longer trust any traffic on your network. The previous model of trusted network internal and untrusted outside your network is over, and everything is untrusted.

One of the best visual examples of ZT was shown to me by John Kindervag himself, leveraging the US presidential motorcade as the visual tool. Much like ZT, the Secret Service trusts no one who approaches the president.

Figure 1.1 shows the presidential motorcade from the 2005 inauguration of President George W. Bush. The protect surface is the oval where the president sits inside the limousine, which is referred to as "the Beast." The Beast has many security features built into it to protect this asset. This is the area ZT is designed to protect—the most valuable asset. The four circles represent the controls around the dotted line of the microperimeter. The pentagon shapes represent the monitoring that is happening around the protect surface, always looking for anomalous behavior coming from anywhere, not just internally or externally; hence, they are facing forward and always looking around the area. The dotted lines on the top and bottom of the picture are the perimeter and clearly show the "firewall" equivalent of the fence. To further illustrate the concept of the protect surface being the focus of ZT, consider a worst-case scenario in which, as a result of an attack on the president, one of the service members who is saluting was injured, but the ZT strategy worked and the president came out unharmed. While it would be tragic if the service member were killed or injured, the mission of ZT was successful. Take the analogy to your environment: Your ZT strategy will be considered successful if during a cyber event your customer database with credit card numbers is unseen and unmolested but you lose public data that was not inside the protect surface.

FIGURE 1.1 U.S. Presidential Motorcade and Security related to Zero Trust

1. Secure Resources For Zero Trust to work as a strategy, it is critical to ensure all resources are accessed securely, regardless of location, and regardless of where the traffic originates to access the resources. You should treat all traffic as a threat, until it is determined to be authorized, inspected, and secured. For example, all traffic should be encrypted, regardless of whether it is internal or external. Insider abuse is often the largest cyber threat organizations face. All traffic, both internal and external, must be inspected for malicious activity and authorized to access the resources. However, it isn't just the access; the level of access must be more specific, via a least-privileged strategy with strictly enforced access controls.

2. Least Privilege and Access Control   The principle of *least privilege* grants users or systems the smallest amount of access to resources needed to perform their tasks. Nothing more, nada. Using this is a standard ZT practice, and users and systems should be offered permissions only when required to perform their duties. Providing users or systems permissions beyond the scope of their requirements can allow them to gain access or change data. I intentionally used the term *users or systems* here because although users are typically associated with people, much of the data access is carried out by systems such as computers, software, or code. These accounts often have excessive privileges or access beyond what they actually need for their intended functions.

An example of why and how, in a nontechnical scenario, is if you ask a neighbor to watch your house while you're away on vacation. The level of work required of the neighbor dictates the level of access provided. For example, if you just want the neighbor to check your mailbox, you give them only the mailbox key, not your house key. However, if you need them to water your indoor plants and walk your dog, you must give them a housekey. Perhaps you don't want them to check the mail but just your houseplants and dog; in this case, you give them only the house-key, not the mailbox key. Further, when you're not on vacation, you don't allow the neighbor to keep keys because they do not need them.

Here is an example of how this should work with a system. A print server accepts print jobs from the local network and copies the documents into a spool directory, which then uses that to print to the paper. When the printer finishes with the printing, it should surrender the right to access that file/spool directory because it no longer needs that resource (until the next print request). One of the most infamous violations is in Internet mail servers (sendmail is a great example), where they require root access to initially gain access to port 25, the classic Simple Mail Transfer Protocol (SMTP) port. Once access to port 25 is completed, the mail server should relinquish that root level access. However, if it does not because it is not required or coded to follow least privilege, an attacker could still leverage that root level access. The server could be tricked into running code at the root level, and anything the attacker attempts will succeed at this level of access.

Access controls must be strict and based on minimal privilege. Currently, the best method for implementing such access controls is with role-based controls for all, employees and third parties. Role-based access controls (RBAC) are standard and best practice, with most software, infrastructure, and IAM systems designed with this in mind. The roles are defined by the minimum level of access required, and users or systems are placed into these roles as a method to ensure access control is enforced. For example, access to a company's finance system has many different roles, and thus permissions or abilities: the analyst who works on Accounts Receivable only has access to A/R, whereas the Chief Financial Officer has access to all of the financial records; the System Administrator has access only to the system configuration for the finance software but not any of the financial records themselves. The backup system that takes nightly snapshots of the database in the finance software only has access to stop the processing of the software so it can safely back up the system without more processing going on.

Privileged users, those with administrator or root level access, can do a lot of damage, both intentionally and accidentally. Malicious actors always strive to get these user accounts so that they can more easily steal data, wreck systems, and plant malicious code. These accounts need to be managed by Privileged Identity

Management (PIM), which allows visibility into their activities and has these super users check out much stronger passwords than a human can process in order to reduce the risk.

Last but not least is governance as part of the overall process for access controls. Cyber governance is all the methods and tools used by an organization to respond to cybersecurity risks, including policies, processes, and programs. NIST describes governance as "the policies, procedures, and process to manage and monitor the organization's regulatory, legal, risk, environmental, and operational requirements are understood and inform management of cybersecurity risk."[3] If there is no governance structure over what is being done to secure information systems, then it is not a repeatable process, and failure is inevitable.

PAM and PIM

Identity and access management (IAM) strategies and tools are part of almost every organization's standard practices. IAM is a term used to describe all the items around user identities, user authentications, and access controls to resources. Privileged access management (PAM) and privileged identity management (PIM) are subsets of the IAM strategy and tools. PIM policies enable controlling elevated privileged users to modify settings, perform provision and deprovisioning of access, and make other changes to user access. PIM solutions also offer the capability to monitor privileged user behavior and access to prevent users from having too many permissions that violate

continues

---

[3]National Institute of Standards and Technology (NIST) Cybersecurity Framework (CSF), www.nist.gov/
cyberframework/identify#:~:text=Governance%20(ID.,the%20management%20of%20
cybersecurity%20risk

(continued)

least-privilege rules. PAM is the process of controlling and monitoring privileged access to resources. PAM solutions manage credentials, provide just-in-time access, and authenticate users. These tools also provide session monitoring and access logs for consumption and alerts. PAM addresses how to monitor and control access when a user requests access to a resource, whereas PIM addresses the access the privileged user already has been granted. Understanding the distinction between PIM and PAM is helpful, even though you'll find that many people confuse them and sometimes use them interchangeably.

3. Ongoing Monitoring and Validation In the old model of chewy centers, most organizations focused on monitoring traffic primarily from external interfaces. In the ZT model, the requirement is to monitor all internal and external traffic. Whether it's the malicious insider or an attacker who broke into your crunchy center, internal monitoring is the only way to detect and remediate any harmful behavior. This monitoring is continuous and ensures the ability to identify suspicious activity by users. Many systems are logged internally by most organizations, but the major difference in ZT is that these are not just logged and reviewed later. Many tools are available that can consume logs in near real time to be able to react more quickly.

Network analysis and visibility (NAV) is a term coined by Forrester in 2011[4] to describe the tools to passively analyze network traffic for threats by leveraging behavior- and signature-based algorithms, to analyze traffic flows, packet captures, and

[4]John Kindervag, "Network Analysis and Visibility," Forrester, Jan 24, 2011; www.forrester.com/report/pull-your-head-out-of-the-sand-and-put-it-on-a-swivel-introducing-network-analysis-and-visibility/RES58445

relationship between assets, to integrate with controls to remediate threats, and to enable forensics. NAV products sit at the center of the network to provide visibility into lateral movement, anomalous behavior, application dependencies, and granular reporting. Other names for these types are network visibility, detection, and response (NVDR) and network traffic analysis (NTA). Regardless of the name, they all use a combination of machine learning, behavior modeling, and rules-based analysis to detect anomalous or malicious activities.

These tools and systems provide key benefits for the ZT strategy. Most importantly, they provide insight into the traffic flow on the network, along with user access and behavior. This is in contrast to the practice of monitoring all applications individually, which in most organizations is not scalable. Given that all applications must work with traffic on the network for access, this approach allows the review of application access and user behavior more holistically and at scale. There is an ability to correlate data for earlier and better breach detection when leveraging NAV, and it sends a message to would-be malicious actors that they are being watched. Think of it as a police car that is following a bad actor down the road: when a driver sees a police car in their rear-view mirror, their driving vastly improves.

Home Depot Data Breach

One of the best examples of a third-party breach—and where ZT would've vastly reduced or eliminated the impact—was the Home Depot breach in 2014. The total bill for Home Depot, as of 2021, was estimated at over $200 million;[5] they were still paying out damages more than 7 years later. The cyberattack was the result of user

continues

---

[5]ArcTitan, "Cast Study: Home Depot Data Breach Cost $179 Million," by News, www.arctitan.com/blog/case-study-data-breach-cost-home-depot-179-million

(continued)

credentials stolen from a vendor of Home Depot that were used to access, then elevate privileges, resulting in the theft of 50 million credit card numbers and 53 million customer email addresses. The attack went on for 5 months, from April 2014 to September 2014, while the hackers moved laterally and undetected as they searched for and found the point-of-sale (POS) system.

Zero Trust Concepts and Definitions

The three key concepts laid out by John Kindervag and adopted into the ZT strategy are the foundation for the tactics and operations success. Because people with a variety of cyber skills may be reading this book, we need to spend a few minutes discussing some key concepts and tactics for implementing ZT.

Multifactor Authentication *Multifactor authentication* (MFA) refers to using two or more factors in authentication. The types of factors can be something you know, something you have, and something you are. Increasingly, a fourth factor is where you are. MFA is not a username and password (which is considered single-factor authentication).

- **Something you know:** Something only the user knows (password or PIN)
- **Something you have:** Any physical object the user has (security token, bank card, key)
- **Something you are:** A physical characteristic of the user (fingerprint, voice, typing pattern, eye)

MFA enhances security because it greatly reduces the risk that an attacker can get access by using just a single factor, such as username and password. Many passwords are reused and are for sale by criminals on the dark web, making a username and password an easy bar to overcome in most cases. A *true* deployment of MFA must use two of the three distinct factors of authentication, not just multiple instances of one factor.

Microsegmentation   *Microsegmentation* refers to the concept of breaking up your network into many zones, thereby limiting the damage that can be done when one area becomes compromised. Segmenting your network can prevent lateral movement from one infected area into the rest of the network. Microsegmentation creates secure areas in the environment to isolate work and data by having firewall policies and policy enforcement points that limit east-west traffic and prevent lateral movement in order to contain breaches and strengthen compliance. It works by expressly allowing specific application or user traffic and, by default, denying all other traffic. Creating granular control policies allows enforcement across any workload (virtual machines, containers).

Typically, in the past, networks were segmented using virtual local area networks (VLANs) and access control lists (ACLs), but microsegmentation takes this a step further by having policies that apply to individual workloads for better attack resistance. Intrusion prevention systems (IPSs), traditional firewalls, and data loss prevention (DLP) usually inspect traffic going north-south (horizontal) in a network. Microsegmentation reduces the blast area of an attack with east-west (lateral) limits that provide better control of communications between systems (servers), which often bypass perimeter-based security tools. This concept allows the tailoring of security settings to different types of traffic and policies that limit traffic from network and applications to those that are expressly permitted.

The goal of microsegmentation is to decrease the attack surface. Segmenting rules all the way down to the workload or application can greatly reduce the risk of a hacker moving from one compromised area or application to another. Operational efficiencies are also gained in this process, as ACLs, router rules, firewall policies, and other systems can become overwhelmed and produce a lot of churn.

Protect Surface The protect surface is the smallest possible reduction of the attack surface and is where the sensitive resources are located. In the old model, the attack surface was often poorly defined as the whole of your network and all resources and assets on it. Defining what is most sensitive and what requires protection and placing that in the protect surface minimizes the attack surface to an easily defined space. This allows the controls to be moved close to the protect surface where the anomalous or malicious activity must be detected. Each protect surface should contain a single resource (DAAS, discussed in the following section), and each ZT environment will have more than one protect surface.

For the context of this book, the protect surface is focused on third parties and their DAAS in your network. ZT is an iterative process that suggests you start with one asset and add to the ZT strategy defined as a new DAAS. Starting with your third-party risk, which are mathematically more likely to have an event, is ideal.

Data, Applications, Assets, Services (DAAS) Data, applications, assets, and services—known as DAAS—are the sensitive resources inside the protect surface. Data is any information that would be damaging if observed or exfiltrated and sits above your organization's risk appetite for loss. Applications are ones that use confidential data or control critical infrastructure or assets.

Assets are devices and organizational and information technologies. Services are those your organization depends on to operate and can include all the back-office operations, such as DNS, DHCP, NTP, and APIs.

The Five Steps to Deploying Zero Trust

The implementation of ZT should be broken down into small, manageable components. As with any large and ongoing effort, it is best to start small and add protect surfaces and sensitive assets as they are identified and remediated in risk-based order. The five steps defined in the process allow the organization to start small and include defining the protect surface, mapping transactions flows, building the ZT architecture, creating the ZT policy, and then monitoring and maintaining the network.

Step 1: Define the Protect Surface   Identify the DAAS that need to have a protect surface defined. Providing a precise definition of this is almost impossible, as it depends on which critical DAAS examples are in your network and on your risk appetite. However, examples include a customer database with Social Security numbers, an application systemically critical to operations, the server running directory services for your domain, or an API that is crucial for your daily close of financial records. There should be only one DAAS asset per protect surface, and your network will have multiple protect surfaces. This step begs a risk-based approach and will take negotiations, but it must be business-driven, not dictated by information security risk alone.

Step 2: Map the Transaction Flows   ZT requires knowledge of how data is flowing in the network—more importantly, in and out and around the protect surface designated in Step 1. As the data flow is understood in relation to the protect surface, it will inform the design of where controls need to be placed. There are various ways to accomplish this task. Often flow diagrams are created as part of existing architecture programs (Step 3). Place a next-generation firewall (transparently passing traffic) and analyze the traffic logs. Many companies sell software or hardware to accomplish this goal.

Step 3: Build the Zero Trust Architecture   Architecture comprises the standards and designs used to meet your strategic, tactical, and operational goals. For example, the architecture should include a requirement for MFA for all privileged access or segmentation gateways to connect and protect networks and enforce Layer 7 policies. Some of the activities in this step are to design a microperimeter in Layer 7 around the attack surface, to concentrate security capabilities into a single control point for all traffic in and out of the protect surface, and to always work to get the controls as close to the protect surface as possible.

Step 4: Create the Zero Trust Policy   This step can be considered the implementation phase of ZT. You've discovered the assets that need protection, mapped the traffic flows, and built standards and designs for an architecture. This information enables the Layer 7 policy creation to enable ZT. Use the Kipling Method to determine which policies need to be followed for access to the DAAS resources behind the protect surface. This access should include users and services (non-people).

Kipling Method of ZT Policy Creation The Kipling Method derives from Rudyard Kipling's 1902 poem "Just So Stories," which reads:

I keep six honest serving men

(They taught me all I knew);

Their names are What and Why and When

And How and Where and Who.

This method has been used for decades to perform problem solving and project planning. One of the challenges in deploying a ZT policy is the creation of policies and what attributes to include. These policies and attributes are the who, what, when, why, and how of resource access requests. The Kipling Method leverages Layer 7 traffic monitoring and determines which traffic is allowed or restricted at the microperimeter around the protect surface.

- Who should have access to the resource? The asserted and validated identity will be defined in this *who* question. Use a user ID system to identify users and enable better control of resource access.

- What application is the resource accessing once the asserted identity is allowed? The protect surfaces are accessed over an application, and this traffic must be validated at Layer 7. Create a way to track application identity via a policy to track applications, and the policy acts in place of the old port and protocol access on traditional firewall rules.

- When is the asserted identity allowed to access the resource?

Leaving access at 24/7 for resources is often unnecessary (when compared to actual required use times) and opens the resource for exploitation during those traditionally nonbusiness hours. Rules should be time-limited and turned off when users would not typically need to access a resource.

- Where is the resource located? Where is the protect surface—for example, in the cloud or on premises?

- Why is the user allowed to access the resource? Using metadata tagging, it is possible to track packets with sensitive data or systems. The metadata can be leveraged by controls and automate policy decisions. Tag data as Toxic or Sensitive to ensure that controls know which data to secure inside the protect surface.

- How should the traffic be processed as it accesses the resource? This defines the criteria used to allow the asserted identity access (the *who* statement) to a resource.

Step 5: Monitor and Maintain the Network   This step provides information to significantly lowers the risk of events and important security data to improve and mature over time. Inspect and log all traffic with decryption done as much as can be processed by the gateway. Logs should be forwarded to a central monitoring software or system. Because zero trust is an iterative process, logging and inspecting all traffic to Layer 7 will improve network security over time, and each subsequent zero trust deployment will be more robust.

Once you've completed the first steps on your first protect surface, the next DAAS asset (in risk-based order) can move through the list of data, applications, assets, or services in an organization's legacy network into a zero trust network.

Zero Trust Frameworks and Guidance

A number of government agencies provide guidance and frameworks on ZT. The National Institute of Standards and Technology (NIST), the Department of Defense (DoD), the National Security Administration (NSA), the Cybersecurity and Infrastructure Security Agency (CISA), and the Office of Management and Budget (OMB) have all published documentation on this subject. They all differ slightly in their scope, ZT definition, and tenets/pillars.

NIST SP 800-207: Zero Trust Architecture, published in August 2020, is the foundation of many other US federal ZT guidelines and provides the roadmap to deploy ZT in the enterprise. It defines ZT as "a cybersecurity paradigm focused on resource protection and the premise that trust is never granted implicitly but must be continually evaluated."[6]

Department of Defense (DoD) Zero Trust Reference Architecture, published in February 2021, is a roadmap of the security features and controls the DoD plans to deploy to achieve its ZT strategy. Borrowing from NIST SP 800-207, the DoD defines ZT as "an evolving set of cybersecurity paradigms that move defenses from static, network-based perimeters to focus on users, assets, and resources."[7]

The NSA's *Embracing a Zero Trust Security Model*, published in February 2021, details the ZT model, its benefits, and its implementation challenges. The NSA provides a slightly different definition of ZT: "a security model, a set of system design principles, and a coordinated cybersecurity and system management strategy based on an acknowledgement that threats exist

---

[6]NIST, *SP 800-207: Zero Trust Architecture*, August 2020, https://csrc.nist.gov/publications/detail/sp/800-207/final

[7]DoD, Zero Trust Reference Architecture, February 2021, https://dodcio.defense.gov/Portals/0/Documents/Library/(U)ZT_RA_v1.1(U)_Mar21.pdf

both inside and outside traditional network boundaries." Their three tenets have become very popular in discussing ZT:

- Never trust, always verify (in contrast to trust, but verify)
- Assume breach
- Verify explicitly[8]

The CISA's *Zero Trust Maturity Model*, published in 2023, provides a way for an agency or organization to assess its current maturity level in ZT and provides a roadmap to improve maturity. Like the DoD, the CISA borrows its definition of ZT from NIST: "Zero Trust provides a collection of concepts and ideas designed to minimize uncertainty in enforcing accurate, least privilege per-request access decisions in information systems and services in the face of a network viewed as compromised."[9]

The OMB's *Federal Zero Trust Strategy: Moving the U.S. Government Toward Zero Trust Cybersecurity Principles* provides a common roadmap for federal agencies, with a requirement to be met by the end of 2024. Their definition takes a tenet from the DoD architecture: "The foundational tenet of the Zero Trust Model is that no actor, system, network, or service operating outside or within the security perimeter is trusted."[10]

The National Security Telecommunications Advisory Committee's (NSTAC) *Zero Trust and Trusted Identity Management*, published in February 2022, provides an overview of the opportunity presented by ZT adoption by US departments and agencies, summarizes best practices and deployment models, and provides recommendations on technologies to be leveraged as

---

[8]National Security Agency (NSA), Embracing a Zero Trust Security Model, February 2021, https://media.defense.gov/2021/Feb/25/2002588479/-1/-1/0/CSI_EMBRACING_ZT_SECURITY_MODEL_UOO115131-21.PDF
[9]Cybersecurity & Infrastructure Security Agency (CISA), Zero Trust Maturity Model 2.0, www.cisa.gov/zero-trust-maturity-model
[10]OMB, *M-22-09: Moving the U.S. Government Toward Zero Trust Cybersecurity Principles*, The White House, January 26, 2022, www.whitehouse.gov/wp-content/uploads/2022/01/M-22-09.pdf

well as a number of recommendations on how the federal government can influence the commercial and nongovernmental adoption of ZT. The document defines ZT as "a cybersecurity strategy premised on the idea that no user or asset is to be implicitly trusted. It assumes that a breach has already occurred or will occur, and therefore, a user should not be granted access to sensitive information by a single verification done at the enterprise perimeter. Instead, each user, device, application, and transaction must be continually verified."[11]

Zero Trust Enables Business

Many organizations have already broken the traditional perimeter model with cloud and/or colocation deployments in which the perimeter no longer has a "crunchy" exterior. Vendor connections and vendor's with your sensitive data further prove this perimeter no longer exists. ZT enables businesses to deploy solutions securely and with more agility because it is data- and identity-centric. Leveraging microperimeters and other key concepts allows for cybersecurity to better support business needs and agility for future requests.

Cybersecurity and Third-Party Risk

Cybersecurity and third-party risk (CTPR) overlap in important ways that are still maturing in many sectors of the economy. A majority of organizations still self-report that they have an ad hoc or no formal process around CTPR due diligence and due care. The first step in having a successful ZT deployment is a

[11]National Security Telecommunications (NSTAC) Advisory Committee, "Zero Trust and Trusted Identity Management," Feb. 2022, www.cisa.gov/sites/default/files/publications/NSTAC%20Report%20to%20the%20President%20on%20Zero%20Trust%20and%20Trusted%20Identity%20Management.pdf

developed and operating CTPR program that has key elements such as systems of record where vendor information is stored.

What Is Cybersecurity and Third-Party Risk?

CTPR, as described in my first book, *Cybersecurity & Third-Party Risk: Third Party Threat Hunting* (Wiley, 2021) is a cyber-focused third-party risk management (TPRM) program. Although that may sound obvious, many organizations do not give sufficient attention to cyber risks. There are more than a few risk domains in most TPR programs: financial, country, credit, ESG (environment, social, and governance), technology, fourth party, resilience, privacy, compliance, legal, and the list goes on.

> Most companies should have, at most, only 6 to 10 risk domains in play at any one time. Having any more than this will immensely slow down due diligence and due care processes without gaining any real risk-reduction benefit. You can limit your number of risk domains in a few ways. First, you want to define your really critical risk domains and not exceed the 6 to 10 limit. Any risk domain not within those first 10 (or whatever number you choose less than that) is then not a risk domain within your TPRM program. Review this decision every year or two to ensure another risk domain hasn't crept up in importance. The second way to lower your number of risk domains is to have delegates. For example, the cybersecurity risk domain can perform due diligence and due care as a delegate for several other risk domains: technology, resilience, fourth party, and potentially privacy, compliance, and country. The first three risk domains are within the cybersecurity CIA triad (confidentiality, integrity, and availability). The last three would need a tighter partnership with the respective domains because there isn't a complete CIA overlap for some areas. Perhaps a risk-based approach would work, where if the vendor is a high-risk third party, the cybersecurity delegate engages directly with those three domain owners to ensure alignment on risk.

The assertion is not that the cybersecurity risk domain is more important than any other risk domains or they are less critical to TPR management success. However, the cybersecurity risk domain stands out as one of the few where an incident with a third party, which is inevitable (not a matter of if), consistently impacts and extends beyond the boundaries of the cybersecurity risk domain into other risk domains. When a third party reports a breach that affects a loss of a large amount of your customer data, it will hemorrhage into financial, legal, privacy, compliance, regulatory, and potentially fourth party, credit and more. It not only affects these risk domains. When the events are large enough, they suck up a ton of these teams' time and resources. In these events, there is a large amount of senior and engineering employee time taken to triage, then investigate, and finally for the postmortem. Add on the time spent by internal and external attorneys, senior executives explaining to investors and the board, and then the regulators come asking your teams what they did wrong to miss such an obvious risk. For shame! No shortage of time sinks will be created by these events.

In addition to the substantial *blast radius*, a term commonly used in cybersecurity circles to convey the extensive range of effects resulting from an event, it is crucial to consider the significant impact on other risk domains and resource allocation. Furthermore, it is worth noting that cybersecurity activity has surged by over 800 percent compared to pre-COVID levels. If you're in this field, the sheer number of security incidents and breaches is apparent in the constant stream of daily alerts and news updates, often involving not just one, but multiple incidents within a single day. The risk is further raised because we've seen an increase in advanced persistent threat (APT) actors in the third-party space. SolarWinds and Colonial Pipeline were the work of these types of threat actors, who have all the time and money to get what they target. SolarWinds was long in the planning by the APT actor; they did tests and even backed out their malicious code to hide the hack for a long time.

This book will build upon the foundation of a cyber-focused TPRM program, aiming to significantly lower the cybersecurity risk by leveraging ZT principles and skills. The primary purpose of ZT is to greatly reduce the blast area, addressing a crucial requirement within the realm of cybersecurity and TPR.

Overview of How to Start or Mature a Program

Starting this section, I highly recommend the purchase of my first book, *Cybersecurity & Third-Party Risk: Third Party Threat Hunting* (Wiley, 2021) and leverage it for how to start or mature a cybersecurity-focused TPRM program. Not only does it provide much more detail on this subject, but the book contains examples and real-world cases to illustrate the risks better. However, the following subsections break it down for those wanting to plow ahead.

Start Here   Where to start is a common question. If you have no cybersecurity and/or a TPRM program, that is a logical question, given that nothing exists. The best place to start is to find out what your risk is, and that starts by compiling an inventory. You want to identify all your third-party entities, categorizing them by vendors, and further delineating the specific services or products they offer. Sometimes a vendor provides more than one service or product. Decide on a system of record (SoR) to store this data, anything from a spreadsheet to expensive, customized software-as-a-solution (SaaS). Regardless, the focus is not on the tools but on the process. Tools can be expensive paperweights if they are not backed up by repeatable processes.

Once you have an inventory in an SoR, you want to then determine which risk domains require due diligence and due care. This book focuses on the cybersecurity risk domain. Within this domain, certain criteria serve as triggers for engaging in CTPR management. Here are two key triggering factors: vendors who will have access to or process sensitive data, and vendors with a connection to your network. In this context, *sensitive data* refers to the data classification levels that your organization views as requiring protection. Cybersecurity due diligence is crucial when a vendor has a connection to your network. Because a connection is an open hole into the network, you should vet all such vendors.

Go through that inventory of vendors to decide which of them hit the criteria set for requiring cybersecurity due diligence and/or due care. This process should also include an analysis of level of risk. For example, who are the high- versus low-risk vendors. Decide on your thresholds for high-, medium-, and low-risk vendors for cybersecurity. A recommended approach is to have an additional level of *systemically critical*, which are defined by business leadership and TPRM leadership as required for the business to operate. You should limit this vendor list to those third parties that would severely or critically impact your business if they were to go down. Risk thresholds below this level can be done on amount of data and type of data. For example, a vendor with 3 million customer records and a vendor with 3,000 customer records represent vastly different risks to the organization. Also consider the type of data: it takes only one network map of your network to be a high risk, or one could have 30 high-value customers that account for over 50 percent of your income. And a vendor with a connection should be considered high risk due to the possibility of an incident on their network traversing to your organization's network.

Intake, Questions, and Risk-Based Approach Once the inventory of your organization's third parties is completed and sorted by risk, the next step is to stand up and document a process that defines how to perform intake due diligence, what follow-up questions are asked, and how to define a risk-based approach. On intake, design a process to sort (like done on existing vendors in the preceding subsection) new vendors or new services/products from existing vendors if they require cybersecurity due diligence and due care. Criteria should be simple to understand and short in length at this step. If the criteria for cybersecurity engagement is that the vendor has sensitive data or a connection to your network, the following few intake questions focus on those risks:

- Will the vendor have access to sensitive customer or employee data? If so, how much volume will be retained?
- Will the solution be hosted outside the company network?
- How critical is the service?
- Will this vendor have access or connect to the company's network? If so, describe connectivity.
- Will any of this be operated offshore?
- Does this vendor require a fourth party (their third party) to deliver service/product to our company?

Any yes answers to these would likely trigger a requirement to perform cybersecurity due diligence and/or due care.

A risk-based approach in this process is to focus on items such as volume of data, service criticality, and connectivity (for example) to determine level of risk. Determining level of risk at intake will do wonders for focusing the team correctly on high-risk vendors versus low-risk ones. Do not treat all vendors the same; they do not present the same risk. To play on an old saying, don't treat everything like a nail just because you think you're a hammer. Some vendors require only a light tap with a tack hammer, whereas others require a 50-pound sledgehammer or even a jackhammer to get all the due diligence and due care completed. That level of work should be based on the level of risk to the organization.

Remote Questionnaires   The most common form of questions provided to vendors is the remote questionnaire. This is the list of cybersecurity (and other risk domains) questions that require the vendor to fill in the answer. These are the bane of both the vendor and your organization because they are often too long and asked too often. The question sets for cybersecurity and technology should be no more than 150 to 200 questions. Any more than that and you risk vendor fatigue and resultant incorrect answers. If your organization is adhering to the NIST Cybersecurity Framework (NIST-CSF), follow each domain and ask which are the important controls for each. Do not ask the same question twice and do not ask questions that will not produce a good window into the vendor's security.

Remote questionnaires are the equivalent of asking your children if their room is clean. Nearly every child in the world will answer yes. However, as we know, as either parents or being a kid ourselves at one point, the definition of *clean* is the rub. The questions should be asked from the perspective of someone who is not inspecting the room but is instead asking their kids about the room's cleanliness. Vendors considered more risky will have someone physically check the room to make sure it is clean, like a parent inspecting their child's room. One suggestion is to use automation for the remote questionnaires of lower-risk vendors. This way you can have a tool review the answers and only send for review the ones that do not have the expected answer or that have the wrong answer. You can use this approach for the high-risk vendors, but this tooling is especially important for lower-risk vendors to ensure less human time is wasted.

Contract Controls   While not a cybersecurity control, you want vendors to comply with cybersecurity terms and conditions (T&Cs) that meet your organization's criteria for due care. These controls hold your vendor to terms that ensure your organization's data and connectivity are properly secured; if they are not, the T&Cs allow legal recourse to go after the third party. Typical controls in this space are encryption, access controls, supplier relationship management, vulnerability management, software development security, network security, data retention, data security, and any other security domains your company has determined to require vendor actions. One recommendation in this area is to identify your critical controls; your team will decide which ones are worth fighting for with a vendor. Here is a short sampling of critical controls:

- Must have cybersecurity program
- Protected data must be at AES-256 equivalent or above
- MFA must be used for all privileged accounts
- Must have logging and monitoring
- Must have a DLP program

- If developing software, must have a secure development life cycle (SDLC)
- Must allow physical validation if risk criteria met

The preceding list shows fewer than 10 items and focuses primarily on the controls listed in New York Department of Financial Services (NYDFS) as required, but it is a good list for any organization as critical controls. This list can be used at the far left of the process, on intake, when a new vendor is going through that process. If they cannot meet any of these seven critical controls, a conversation should happen with business leadership regarding the risk of proceeding with this third party.

Physical Validation   The act of physically validating security controls at the third party is the *gold standard* for security assessments. This involves your organization requiring the vendor to demonstrate not only policy and process documentation for security but also that these are in production and assurance that work is being done. Prior to COVID, this was often called *onsite validation*. Post-COVID, this can be successfully accomplished with collaboration tools (virtual physical validation), but that still leaves a physical validation of their physical security. Vendors with a cloud service provider (CSP) such as AWS or Azure, or a vendor with lower risk, are perfect candidates for the virtual physical validation because they do not have a data center of their own to tour and validate. When third parties have their own data center (or are higher risk) or when your data is stored in a colocation data center, onsite physical validation is best. Data centers run by vendors can be risky places. Data centers are expensive, and over time a third party may decide to skimp on maintenance or needed security upgrades due to this cost. If the risk of the vendor is tolerable for your risk appetite and it has its own data center, best to go and check the vendor yourself.

For this process, you want to develop a questionnaire that is conversational, not a checklist. Checklists are notorious for not producing a security assessment, but instead just providing a compliance exercise. Compliance is not security. Asking questions about security domains, and then asking for evidence it is running in production, produces more information than a checklist. For example, based on the NIST-CSF, the team can ask about the vendor's access management domain. Start by asking if the third party has an access management policy or standard. Having a policy, standard, and process documentation shows a repeatable process has at least been established and documented. Second, ask the vendor to demonstrate they are reviewing per policy. If the access management policy says they review and update every year, but the document hasn't been touched in several years, that indicates something is missing. Assuming that the third party successfully "passes" the first two steps (they have a policy, and they update it properly), walk through the document. During the process, the cyber assessor gets to the part about password complexity. It states that users must have a minimum of 10 characters and three of the four complexity factors. Here are two ways to determine whether the vendor adheres to this in production: a screenshot of their Active Directory policy or having someone attempt to change their password without following the rules. You can repeat this process for each domain. It provides a great picture of the vendor's security across the enterprise.

Continuous Monitoring The term *continuous monitoring* has a few meanings in the TPR space. For this book, the term refers to the process of monitoring the cybersecurity risks of a vendor in-between the point-in-time assessments (remote questionnaires or physical validation). The point-in-time assessments occur at most once a year, and often it can be several years before the vendor is queried again on their cybersecurity risks. As indicated earlier, the level of cybersecurity activity against third parties is exponentially larger than pre-COVID, and waiting for this assessment is an invitation for an incident.

Take the higher-risk vendors and develop a program to monitor them on an ongoing basis. This goes beyond just the usual remote questionnaires, and instead includes tools and processes to identify risks, correlate them to already known risks with that vendor, and engage them on these specific risks. This is often accomplished by using vendor security rating tools, sometimes provided as a SaaS solution. This software provides a score, either a FICO-type score or letter grade or other relevant scale, to give an overall risk rating for the vendor. These tools are useful, but the "score" is not the item to use in this continuous monitoring process. In this process, use the cybersecurity risks underneath the score in the tool. For example, most of them will indicate open ports, spam propagation, botnet infections, patching cadence, and others. These alerts are where the action begins. Once an alert has fired off for a specific alert, the cyber assessor can research that threat, look at the risk of the vendor internally, and then decide on the next steps. An example process can demonstrate best:

- An alert comes from the vendor security rating tool indicating a botnet infection.
- Assessor researches the botnet and discovers it is a potential keylogger.
- Assessor researches the vendor internal due diligence and due care information.
  - Research indicates vendor has an open risk acceptance for insufficient DLP.
- Assessor determines overall risk of threat and vendor.

- Vendor is high risk, and the botnet is combined with insufficient DLP.
- If threshold reached, assessor contacts the vendor with this information.
  - When the threshold is reached, the assessor has a talk with the vendor about a specific threat (botnet infection with insufficient DLP).

This conversation with the vendor about a specific threat and accompanying lack of proper DLP is much more productive than their overall score on the tool.

Disengagement and Cybersecurity *Vendor offboarding*, or disengagement, refers to the act of terminating a third party's relationship with your organization. This is often the process most overlooked, and the consequences can be devastating for companies. Many of the activities in the disengagement process are easily added to a checklist to ensure no step is missed. First, the most common activity is access security. Physical access must be terminated along with virtual or logical access. Physical access is often overlooked for third parties because people tend to forget that these third parties used to come to their location. Ensure that an access review process exists to catch any third party's physical and virtual removals and any subsequent attempts to log in.

The vendor's connectivity is critical to terminate. A physical connection, such as an MPLS or VPN, can be relatively easy to terminate (because this can be unplugged, literally). The tougher connections to catch are the HTTPS and intermittent (FTP or Box, for example). Collaborate with your network security teams or those running your security information and event management (SIEM); they can capture these connections on an ongoing basis. It will take some investigation, but you should be able to trace these connections to the vendor. Whether your organization uses a safelist or explicitly blocks all connections, these types of traffic must be monitored and stopped when a relationship ends.

Often a relationship is not really over when the line of business declares it so. For example, regulatory or contractual requirements may require retention of a relationship/data for a long period after the contract is terminated. Pay attention to these requirements and ensure all data-retention requirements are met during this disengagement process. If data does not need to be retained, require a certificate of destruction. Be sure to ask for a digital certificate of destruction, if possible, because this provides a lot more detail about how and when the data was destroyed.

Reporting and Analytics   One benefit of creating and maturing a cybersecurity-focused TPRM program is the ability to be more proactive and predictive. Currently, most TPRM teams are very reactionary, waiting for the vendor to call in and report an incident. This is not a good place to be operating from long term. All the due diligence and due care data your team has collected and leveraged to make better TPR decisions can now be turned into a business decision tool. Grab a business intelligence or analytics tool and start feeding this data into it. Not all data is created equally. For example, the physical validation data results are more trustworthy than remote questionnaire results. In your decision tool, ensure the data is weighed correctly to enable good decision making from it. It does not take long for this data to begin to show trends and indicators of how a vendor is doing with regard to cybersecurity risk.

ZT with CTPR

The struggle is real: The pace of third- and fourth-party cyber incidents is not slowing, and organizations are often unsure of what to do to lower this risk. How would an organization get a vendor (or a vendor's vendor, in the case of a fourth party) to perform their own security controls adequately to truly lower the risk of an incident? Even organizations with mature cybersecurity and TPRM programs are still being impacted. Overlaying the ZT principles will not stop the incidents, but it will greatly reduce the risk.

Why Zero Trust and Third-Party Risk?

The introduction has the most direct reason why taking a ZT approach to TPR is "mathematical inevitability." In the current environment, with numerous breaches occurring, it's almost a statistical certainty that most companies, which typically have dozens to thousands of vendors, will experience breaches. ZT assumes a breach and provides a way to greatly reduce the risk when breaches happen.[12] Hence, starting with the area with the highest probability of a breach to reduce the impact makes logical sense.

With all that has been presented about ZT and a cyber-focused TPRM program, it may be obvious why you'd want to pursue a ZT strategy with respect to TPR. ZT's principles, architecture, concepts, journey, strategy, and all are well aligned to vastly lower the damage from a potential third-party breach. ZT assumes a breach has happened or will happen, which given the

---

[12]National Security Telecommunications (NSTAC) Advisory Committee, "Zero Trust and Trusted Identity Management," Feb. 2022, www.cisa.gov/sites/default/files/publications/NSTAC%20Re port%20to%20the%20President%20on%20Zero%20Trust%20and%20Trusted%20Identity%20 Management.pdf

pace of incidents and breaches is a sound (if not depressing) assumption. ZT presents a least-privilege approach to all users, applications, and infrastructure, which is exactly what a CTPR program should be presenting to vendors. ZT requiring all communications to be secured, regardless of location, aligns perfectly with how to protect third-party communications. ZT requires that all resource authentication, authorization, and access are granted on a per-session basis and are dynamic and strictly enforced before access is permitted. Lastly, ZT requires that the enterprise collect and monitor information about assets, network infrastructure, and communications continuously.

All of these tenets of ZT align well with a cyber-focused TPR program. Although we trust vendors, we do so after completing due diligence and due care. The cyber-focused program is designed to be a threat-hunting exercise designed to continuously monitor vendors and ensure they have access to only the data and connectivity they are explicitly allowed. Most importantly, ZT endeavors to reduce the blast area of an incident or breach; lowering the potential damage for a vendor's breach or incident translates into a real risk reduction, not only in cybersecurity risk domain but also in all the others that are affected by a cyber incident: financial, reputational, compliance, legal, and more.

ZT is best done in increments and sprints (it is a journey, remember?). There are many ways to start that journey, but starting with the vendor risk area is a great way to lower the risk for areas not directly under your control with a third party. Third parties are a finite number, but you can narrow it further by taking a risk-based approach and focusing on vendors that meet your risk criteria (that is, have sensitive data or a connection to your network). That number is even smaller and is more easily measured for success or completeness. As an organization identifies the steps needed to complete ZT for third parties, the steps can be further incremented by focusing on systemically critical vendors first in the rollout. This stepped approach is well suited for ZT deployments where the teams design, test, implement, monitor, and adjust as needed.

How to Approach Zero Trust and Third-Party Risk

The challenge for most cybersecurity organizations in performing TPR is that these departments or groups are designed to focus on first party (your own organization). Many cybersecurity teams struggle with third-party due diligence and due care because they are so tuned to their own internal security controls and gaps that getting the same information from a vendor seems nearly impossible. The difference comes when the CTPR teams understand that the same due diligence and due care applied to internal can be applied to external third parties, with a little change in viewpoint.

When performing an internal security assessment, a cybersecurity team will engage with the domain owners and determine the level of security controls. Then they record gaps and come up with a remediation plan to close the gap. In a third-party due diligence effort, the same inquiry process happens, but the subject matter experts (SMEs) are not your peers at the organization. This means the same questions and answers but a different expectation on how the validation is performed. There will need to be more artful discussions, in some cases, than you have with an internal peer because they are not answerable to a manager in your organization. Rather, approach the vendor as a valued partner, remind them that the effort is intended to partner with them to find any potential security gaps, and then work together to develop a remediation plan. That sense of collective engagement with a third party builds trust and a willingness to share, particularly in a physical validation process.

Taking that same approach with ZT and TPR is the key to success. Rather than focus on the first-party (internal) steps to deploy ZT, focus on what a vendor should be doing, or what your internal systems can enforce on third parties, to enable that goal as a strategy. There are three basic areas: users, applications, and infrastructure. For each of these three main pillars, develop a way to implement ZT. Within each of these three pillars, there are four main activities: identity, device/workload, access, and transaction. The word *transaction* used in the following section could be described as monitoring or even condition. The use of transaction is not meant to be misleading, but is focused on what your organization is doing in the monitoring, which is focused on transactions. Focusing on these main activities for each of the pillars is ideal for success because it breaks down this complex process into achievable and measurable bits. This brings us to the OSI model.

ZT/CTPR OSI Model

One of the biggest challenges an organization can have in ZT and TPR is how to mash the two together into a strategy or plan. In 2020, The Identity Defined Security Alliance (IDSA), published a whitepaper titled "Putting Identity at the Center of Security" (www.idsalliance.org/wp-content/uploads/2022/06/IDSA_Framework_Whitepaper-1.pdf) that helps define the problem of space and solutions very well. It led a fellow author, George Finney, to conclude that the Open Systems Interconnection (OSI) model when customized with TPR can help organizations develop an efficient strategy. George created a Zero Trust OSI table in his book "Project Zero Trust" to assist readers in how to implement Zero Trust strategy. Translating this table into a vendor risk viewpoint, it is morphed into the 'Zero Trust and Third-Party OSI Table', as seen in Table 1.1.

TABLE 1.1 Zero Trust and Third-Party OSI Table

	Identity	Device/Workload	Access	Transaction
ZT for TP Users	Validate TP users with strong authorization.	Verify TP user device integrity.	Enforce least-privilege access for TP users to data and apps.	Scan all content for TP malicious activity and data theft.
ZT for TP Apps	Validate TP developers, DevOps, and admins with strong authorization.	Verify TP workload integrity.	Enforce least-privilege access for TP workloads accessing other workloads.	Scan all content for TP malicious activity and data theft.
ZT for TP Infra	Validate TP users with access to infrastructure.	Identify all TP devices (including IoT).	Enforce least-privilege access segmentation for third-party infrastructure.	Scan all content within the infra for TP malicious activity and data theft.

*ZT = zero trust; TP = Third Party

The table is broken down into three rows (by type of resource for ZT) and three columns (by activity performed that requires controls). This table will be the source of many of our decisions about each resource as to how to best lower the risk and blast radius in the event of an incident. Going by row and column:

- **ZT for TP users:** This is any vendor or third party that is accessing your network or accessing your data.
  - **Identity:** Validate users with a strong authentication methodology. Consider enforcing multifactor authentication for all third-party users.
  - **Device/Workload:** Verify that third-party user devices have correct integrity before connecting on network and continuously.
  - **Access:** Have a process defined where third-party users are only given permission to perform their roles, nothing more; ensure access reviews are there to catch any permissions creep.
  - **Transaction:** As work (transactions) are taking place, scan all data and movement of third parties to detect any malicious or out-of-ordinary activity or data exfiltration.
- **ZT for TP applications:** This is any vendor or third party that is accessing your network or accessing your data.
  - **Identity:** Validate third-party developers, DevOps, and privileged account holders have strong authentication and multifactor authentication.
  - **Device/Workload:** All applications running must be scanned to ensure they are running only code allowed and in area of memory allowed.
  - **Access:** Ensure all third-party applications/workloads are only given permissions at the level needed to perform their functionality. Often vendors will require an application to have root level or administrator access and that should not be allowed.

- **Transaction:** As workloads and applications run, systems must be scanning them to find any activity that is suspicious or is leading to data exfiltration.

- **ZT for TP infrastructure:** This is any vendor or third party that is accessing your network or accessing your data.
  - **Identity:** Any device must have strong authentication before being allowed on the network. Pay attention to everything from network equipment to Internet of Things (IoT) devices.
  - **Device/Workload:** Find and catalog all third-party devices on the network, especially IoT devices. It is typical for an organization to have a configuration management database (CMDB) on their own equipment, but this must include any third-party device as well (whether your team manages it or it is a vendor-managed device).
  - **Access:** Least privilege here is on a couple of fronts. First, the permissions a device is allowed must only be at a level needed to perform its role or function (not a root or admin level unless a valid business needs calls for that level of permissions). Second, the access along the wire, or network, must be limited to only those virtual local area networks (VLANs) or other means of microsegmentation required to perform their role or function.
  - **Transaction:** As infrastructure performs its role or function, it must be constantly scanned to observe and react to any malicious behavior or signs that data is being exfiltrated.

This model is simplified, but it allows leadership and individual contributors to see the resource types (users, applications, infrastructure) and how to enable ZT for each of the activities (identity, device/workloads, access, and transactions). These 12 boxes provide a user-friendly process to roll out ZT either row by row, column by column, or even in a tic-tac-toe approach. This gives maximum flexibility to the leadership and deployment/ operations teams as to which items to pick first versus last.

The next chapters go into detail about each of these resource types and activities performed to enable ZT on third parties. Those chapters discuss each of them in detail and provide examples of each type of resource and activity to focus on in the columns.

2

Zero Trust and Third-Party Risk Model

The zero trust (ZT) and third-party risk (TPR) OSI model (Open Systems Interconnection) has been designed to break down complex concepts into simpler understandable "chunks" for organizations to consume easier. Each row and column intersection requires a bit of detail to provide enough material to take action on them. As this chapter goes through each of these intersections, you'll learn more about how they can be successfully navigated as a step along the ZT journey in the TPR space.

Zero Trust and Third-Party Users

The first area in ZT and TPR to focus on is users. In this case, a *user* refers to any resource that is classified as such. This should be focused on an actual person, while the other two resource categories deal with applications and infrastructure. Much of the work in ZT focuses on the identity and access management (IAM) domain, and starting with users is often the easiest (given the risk). When starting off on this exercise, be sure to differentiate between your internal native users and third parties. This sounds obvious, but there could be vendors with an internal login native to your domain. For instance, the third-party user may work for the vendor, but their login is not listed as their vendor's name, rather it is your own organization's name. The vendors with external logins that contain their vendor domain name are easiest to identify, but often access is granted using the native organization's access management system. Ensure those are identified as part of this process. If you are using a federated model for single sign-on (SSO), this will be done using your internal access management system.

Access Control Process

Before discussing the process of authentication, it would be good to provide a refresher on the access control process (authentication being part of these three steps):

1. **Identification:** The process where a resource identifies itself

2. **Authentication:** Verification of a resource's identity

3. **Authorization:** Decision to allow or deny access to an object or resource

These three steps are separate and distinct, and they must happen in this order for the whole access control process to complete. For example, when you want to buy alcohol in a place that requires an access control process to purchase liquor, you will be asked to prove you're old enough. The clerk will ask for identification. You will provide your driver's license, and the clerk will inspect it to ensure you are old enough; that is authentication. Lastly, the clerk will permit the sale of the alcohol to you, and that is authorization.

The most common form of identification in the digital world is a user typing his username or email address to claim the identity of an account. That is the first step of access control. Next in the process, the user typically provides a password to perform authentication (I really am the user that I identified myself as). Multifactor deployment provides another method of authentication such as biometrics or a one-time password (OTP). Authorization enables the user to access the resource; in access to email, this step ensures the user has access to only their email, not other's email. In another case, the user might have been an administrator, and that authorization would provide that privileged user with more access. As the chapter discusses the topic of strong authentication, it is important to remember this is one step in a three-step process.

Identity: Validate Third-Party Users with Strong Authentication

Users are often the "weakest link" in most security breaches. Nearly all the breaches or security incidents in the last 10 years have been due to a user account being compromised. In fact, the Verizon Breach Report for 2022 continues to state that 80 percent of breaches are due to user accounts being inadequately secured. Often, they are compromised because the "user" did not use the best security practices when it came to password complexity and recycling. Most systems users log in with require basic authentication: username and password. But this is the weak link: username and password. Many users recycle the same passwords, and when hackers have stolen almost everyone in the world's usernames and passwords (at this point, it is not much of exaggeration to say it), those credentials eventually may end up on sale on the Dark Web. On any given day, billions of these credentials are for sale in the criminal areas of the Internet. Some are very cheap, at a few U.S. dollars per record, but some cost up to thousands if they are confirmed as a root or administrator account. Basic authentication is not going to be any part of a ZT deployment.

Strong authentication has a few definitions, but this book focuses on three big frameworks or organizations to guide our understanding: NIST 800-63 for overall framework; strong customer authentication (SCA), which is a requirement in the EU; and the Fast Identity Online (FIDO) Alliance, an open industry association that supports a wide range of authentication technologies. The National Institute of Standards and Technology (NIST) defines strong authentication as "A method used to secure computer systems and/or networks by verifying a user's identity by requiring two-factors in order to authenticate (something you know, something you are, or something you have)." The Federal Financial Institutions Examination Council (FFIEC) by adding the requirement that both factors cannot be from the same category (example, both cannot be something you are) but must be from separate categories. The Cloud Security Alliance (CSA) defines strong authentication as "an authentication based on the use of two or more elements categorized as knowledge (something only the user knows), possession (something only the user possesses), and inherence (something the user is) that are independent in that the breach of one does not compromise the reliability of the others and is designed in such a way as to protect the confidentiality of the authentication data." These definitions are fairly similar, and so to enable strong authentication there needs to be deployment of a multifactor authentication (MFA) and/or strong authentication. The following sections delve into the different types of strong authentication and provide more details on each.

Five Types of Strong Authentication   Five types of strong authentication exist.

One-Time Passwords   One-time passwords (OTPs) are verification codes most often sent to your phone via SMS or text. As the term implies, the code is only available for use a single time and most often with a time limit on how long it is valid. There is a subcategory or type, which is the application-generated OTP. These are often seen in online applications that generate the passcode for use on that particular application only. This type also includes a specialized authentication application such as Microsoft Authenticator or similar.

Biometrics   Biometrics are generally considered as the strongest of the authentication methods. They are very hard to hack, but one drawback is the difficulty of tuning a biometric system. Biometrics also require the deployment of biometric hardware-capable devices. The most common types of biometrics include:

- **Fingerprint:** This is the most common type of biometric, and some laptops come equipped with them built in.
- **Eye scanner:** Hardware for this is not as widely available, and it can be prone to inaccuracies if a person has contacts or wears glasses.
- **Facial recognition:** Matches facial characteristics. Facial recognition has been seen to show some spoofing by close

relatives, but generally it is considered a robust type of biometric.

- **Typing recognition:** This requires the user to type in a phrase, and the system matches the user's typing style, which is unique for people. Software does require training and is not widely deployed at this time.

- **Speaker recognition:** Voice biometrics use speech patterns to authenticate. They usually rely on standardized words to identify users, much like a password.

Certificate-Based Authentication   Certificate-based authentication uses a digital certificate to identify users, machines, or devices. The certificate contains a digital identity of the resource (in this case, a user) with a public key and the digital signature of the certificate authority that issued it. A user provides a digital signature when signing in; Active Directory verifies the credibility of the digital signature and the certificate authority. Then the system cryptographically validates that the user has the correct private key associated with the certificate. A common deployment of this is via email, when a sender digitally signs the message, which allows the recipient to verify the signature and know for sure the message was sent by the actual sender.

Token-Based Authentication   If you have ever used a USB device or smartcard plugged into a laptop to log in to a system, you likely used a token-based system. A token-based system allows users to enter their credentials once and get a string of random characters in exchange for access to the system.

Multifactor Authentication   MFA requires two or more independent ways to identify a resource or user. It can leverage many of the authentication methods described above (biometrics or OTP), and MFA is considered a very good defense against account hacking. It should be deployed for any remote access or internal access to sensitive or protected areas. Note that MFA alone is not enough because there have been instances where it has been compromised due to social engineering or what is called *push fatigue*. Push fatigue refers to users getting frustrated with all the OTPs that get sent to their devices.

These five strong authentication methods must be leveraged for any third-party user requiring access to your network or applications. There can be an initial baby step taken if these five types are not immediately available for deployment to the vendors: Make password complexity and rules much more stringent and difficult. This initial step is not truly strong authentication but can be an acceptable first step prior to using a strong authentication method. Examples would be to enforce longer password length (minimum of 12 characters), have it check for dictionary words or unacceptable or too easy-to-guess passwords, and make complexity (such as passphrases or upper, lower, and characters) more challenging. NIST and others are now recommending strong passwords that never change (or only once a year). This is due to user behavior on the "old" way of changing passwords every 60 or 90 days. Users will often use "cheats" to get around this constant requirement with Password1, Password2, Password3, etc. This defeats the purpose of password rotation and makes them far too easy to guess. Again, none of these qualify for the more secure strong authentication methods listed above, but never let perfection get in the way of progress, as long as there is a milestone to implement MFA and other strong authentication methods for vendors.

> Ensure that your password rules (both on-prem and for vendors) require a minimum age of one day before the password can be changed. This is a common mistake that if not enforced

will allow a user to "game" the password history. Here's an example of how they can do it. If no rule says you have to wait a certain amount of time before changing your password, and your policy is that you can't reuse your last 10 passwords, a user can quickly cycle through those 10 passwords to go back to using their original password. This would defeat the purpose of changing the password for security reasons.

Strong authentication is a key step in securing an identity-based system, but this must be managed by two important technology and process pieces: identity and access management (IAM) and privileged access management (PAM).

Identity and Access Management　IAM ensures the correct resources access only the tools they need to perform their roles. This definition is less expensive than traditionally, prior to when a ZT journey is embarked on. Many tools and products exist, with a wide range of cost options, to manage an enterprise IAM. If you are a small shop, it is perfectly reasonable to do some of this in a size and complexity to fit your risk appetite. However, any of these solutions must fit some basic requirements to perform the needs to implement a successful ZT deployment—in particular, to manage the fine-grain, dynamic identity policies required. Also, items such as limited birthright (static, long-standing permissions), role-based access controls (RBACs), and support of attribute-based access controls (ABAC) lead to dynamic and policy-based access controls.

Separation of Duties　This is part of the granularity requirement in identity for a ZT deployment. The principle is that no one resource should have access to all of an organization's sensitive data or secrets. Access from a VPN is not enough, but they must also limit the access for that resource coming in from a

VPN to only those areas on the network that identity is authorized to access. Also important in this capability is no single resource will have multiple roles. For example, a developer should not have access from tests into production or the ability to self-elevate their privileges.

Least-Privilege Access   The ability to ensure a resource's access can be limited to only those other resources required to perform if their role is key to ZT. The tools and process used must describe and implement access that is limiting by design.

Multifactor Authentication   This critical ability to raise the security level for authentication should be integrated with process and technologies deployed. There will be a heavy reliance on MFA for many resources as they attempt to access more sensitive resources areas, and in some cases they will have to reauthenticate at various times using MFA.

Just-in-Time Access   This is the opposite of the way some systems are designed to stay connected all the time, near permanently. Similar to the least-privilege access, just-in-time access further limits access to only when a resource requires access. When that access is no longer needed (work is completed), the access is revoked until the next time. The ability to be granular in terms of time greatly lowers the risk because it limits the time a hacker can spend causing damage.

Auditing, Logging, and Tracking   The requirement that any IAM process and tools deployed perform logging, auditing, and tracking is last in this list because of its criticality, regardless of the size and complexity of your organization. If there is no logging, auditing, or tracking, ZT cannot be implemented successfully. There are a hundred reasons why this is the key capability, but at a minimum because ZT is a journey that is always building and improving, which cannot be accomplished if these three activities are not being performed.

As ZT processes are developed and technologies deployed to support those processes, having an IAM that delivers these key five capabilities should be the main focus. Because the space of options for tools and technologies is so varied now and can sometimes be sold as the "solution," it's possible to miss that it is more important to have a solid program and process defined first. The tools and technologies should support the goals of the program and process. Focus on the five areas and capabilities in the IAM process and tools to be sure they can deliver the ZT for third parties' goals.

Privileged Access Management   While PAM is part of IAM, this section breaks it down because it plays a special role in a ZT deployment. Because a PAM system, by definition, manages privileged (administrator, root, su, etc.) accounts, this area must be a special area of focus when looking to ZT and TPR. Adding to the risk here is that these are outside (third parties) resources with privileged rights within your organization's resources. Ensuring your team's PAM process and tools are solid is very critical. Remember, Edward Snowden was a contractor for the U.S. government when he stole top secret data. The U.S. government did not limit his access and did not manage his privileged access in the least. There are several types of privileged access management processes and systems.

Traditional PAM   When we say *traditional*, this is meant as "old-school," or could be inferred as "stop doing this soon." The traditional way was to make administrator passwords more complex (more than 12 characters) and have them expire more quickly (every 30 days instead of 90). In one early approach, a password vault is used with a very complex, hashed password that is copy-pasted when required. These early solutions for managing privileged access should not be used because they are far too risky in today's cybersecurity environment.

First-Gen PAM These first-generation solutions took the password vault to the next and more mature stage, where an elevated privileged account is placed in a system that changes the password frequently (usually tuned to several times a day or more), and the resource gets this updated password as required throughout the time they require access to the other resource. A variety of processes and technologies are built around these first-generation products and are great for any deployment of ZT.

PAM in the Cloud PAM in the cloud is very similar to first-generation PAM, but there can be some advantages, given that many organizations are in a hybrid (cloud and on-prem) mode. All the major cloud service providers (CSPs) have solid solutions for hybrid or full-cloud deployments of PAM, along with a vast resource library of program and process solutions to enable a ZT foundation with a strong PAM deployment.

Next-Gen PAM Next-generation PAM systems take away some of the friction caused in the first-gen PAM solutions with administrators having to check in and check out new passwords. These newer solutions leverage short-lived (called ephemeral) certificates that allow the resource to connect securely with one click (or so they claim). These systems are hybrid and support both on-prem and cloud PAM deployments, along with third-party resources, in a single pane of glass. These systems also integrate with your existing Active Directory and other IAM systems. Obviously, if this is the system and process at your organization and it is successfully deployed, you are well positioned to deploy this pillar of ZT. First-gen and PAM in the cloud are all sufficient, and there are hundreds of solutions (process and tools) available.

Session Monitoring Most organizations use the traditional method of authentication, authorization, and access, where it is checked only once (upon the initial entry of the user). In ZT, the IAM infrastructure is designed to be near-continuous monitoring of the sessions. Then based on the risk of the asset being accessed, session monitor may require renewed authentication and authorization on a periodic basis for continued access to the resource or asset.

As this section on how to validate third-party users with strong authentication wraps up, recall that there are three steps in the access control process: identification, authentication, and authorization. There are five types of strong authentication: one-time passwords, biometrics, certificate-based authentication, token-based authentication, and MFA. To ensure your team can deploy ZT identity-based security for resources, the process and tools must support a strong IAM and PAM deployments.

Device/Workload: Verify Third-Party User Device Integrity

Verification of third-party user device integrity means checking the security posture and integrity of the "machine" (PC, laptop, server, microservice, container) that the resource is using to access another resource. Typically, the easiest way to think of this is the following scenarios. A vendor's agent comes to your organization with his corporate laptop. When that laptop attempts to connect to your guest network, is it checked for any malware or botnets that might flood the network? Or an offshore worker connects to perform their daily work for your team. They use their vendor's laptop and connect with a VPN. Is that laptop validated prior to connecting that it is up-to-date and safe to connect? If it is not safe to connect, is there a process to isolate, quarantine, and then resolve the issue that may be preventing work? There are a number of processes and technologies that can be leveraged to successfully check third-party devices for integrity and security.

Checking device integrity should not be confined to laptops and PCs. It must extend to home networking gear used to attach: bring your own device (BYOD) and personal devices, unmanaged devices, VPN infrastructure, servers, network equipment, and printers. Many vendors will place printers in your network, network gear or servers in your data center, or bring in their own corporate infrastructure to perform the function your organization pays them to complete. Think about the broad possibilities, depending on how your needs for vendor-supplied work can vary.

The security of home networks has always been a problem, and now that many technology-based workers can (and do) work remotely, improving the integrity and security of the connectivity to the third-party user's endpoint is even more important. For those who work remotely, and to reduce the risk of bad security in home networks, provide remote workers with a preconfigured home router from your organization (or a third-party provides it to their remote workers). Providing this equipment drastically lowers the lack of control in that "last yard" of connectivity at the vendor's home office. In addition to the physical security risk lowered due to the direct control of the equipment (including updates), the policy can dictate that when the risk makes it needed, the vendor can only connect with this corporate-issued device. This type of restriction would limit them from connecting from another remote location that is less secure: coffee shop, friend's living room, at an airport lounge, etc. Providing these types of equipment to users requires a budget and team to do the project to develop and deploy the technology (along with the process to support it). In addition, the ongoing support requires a resource and monetary commitment. The counter to this negative is that the alternative is far less palatable: a breach due to poor end-user security controls in a hybrid or fully remote environment. Where the risk appetite warrants it, the investment is worth the reward in terms of very low risk of breach or incident for remote users, which is a fact of life in our own organizations and with our third parties.

Ensure device integrity involves looking for device implants, malware code, backdoors, or other items that could give administrative control over the vendor's device. The system should check on initial connection and then at regular intervals on device integrity to ensure that no new malware or implants have been added. More mature deployments will involve checking the device posture, which goes a few steps more and lowers the risk even further. For example, device posture checking will regularly check a device for vulnerabilities, whether from a Common Vulnerabilities and Exposures (CVE) type of connection or based on manufacturer feed. It checks for the signature on the firmware updates to the user's device and validates if the updates were secure and successful. At the user device, it validates the BIOS and UEFI firmware are the correct and signed versions.

Hybrid or remote workers are the most apparent example of how important checking vendor device integrity and posture is. Since COVID, remote or hybrid work has become the norm for many technology-based workers. Those vendors were in the office prior to the remote work model, but now they are all working from home or somewhere else you do not physically control. They are just as likely to be connecting from untrustworthy environments (coffee shops, hotel lobbies, airport terminals). They all connect via VPN and then are trusted to go wherever they want in the network, typically. Even if they are in the relative safety of their home network, many home routers are compromised or poorly maintained, if at all. Who is sniffing their wireless traffic in the next apartment as they connect? All these are great reasons to check that the device they are connecting to your network is secure and stable.

Access: Enforce Least-Privilege Access for Third-Party Users to Data and Apps

This section focuses on vendors who are accessing data or applications as a user account, not privileged account. This user is an account that cannot perform any administrative actions on the system or application. While this type of account cannot do as much damage as a privileged user, limiting access to only what the vendor resource requires to perform their role is a key principle in ZT. Some basic ways to manage least privilege for third-party users is groups, work hours, geo-location, and device-based restrictions.

Groups   Groups are a way to manage privileges for hundreds or thousands of users. In this case, the user groups would be based on vendor access requirements. For example, there could be a vendor group by use case: offshore, sales partner, application development, and benefits administration. Each of these use cases would involve a different type of where the vendor would access from (location), time of day they access, what device they would use to connect, and what other resources they are allowed to access. Clearly define where each of these groups has the right to access and what to access. Offshore workers only have access to the virtual desktop interface (VDI); the sales partner vendors only have access to the product pricing tables and entry of sales numbers; the application development user would have only read access to production (to check work); and the benefits administrator vendor can only interact with the human resources folders and the main HR software on-premises.

Work Hours   As mentioned, each group should have expected work hours to ensure it is least-privileged access. Offshore workers, for a U.S.-based company, could have business process outsourcing (BPO) in India, and their support could be done during nighttime hours in the United States. If there is a login to work during 2 p.m. Eastern Time, the actions can range from complete denial of access, quarantine to remediate, or a warning or flag to appropriate personnel at your organization that there is an attempt to log in outside of normal hours for any member of a group.

Geo-Location   Work is a thing you do, not a place you go. That statement sums up why it is important to make a geographic location part of your restrictions for third-party users. Keeping with the offshore BPO based in India, as an example, the system should be checking from where the user is connecting and validate it is correct for that group. If the vendor's user attempts to connect from Brazil, the system should reject the connection.

Device-Based Restrictions   This last restriction can be a challenge to implement, based on your system ability. However, if the system can check that the vendor is connecting with expected equipment, that is ideal. Examples of why this is important vary from a vendor who services your networking equipment should only connect with a device known to be from them to an offshore vendor connecting only with a VDI.

Creating the groups for vendors and managing the access restrictions for each can start with a large couple of buckets and mature into as many as needed to make it scalable and not cumbersome to manage. There will be exceptions to some of these groups: Perhaps the offshore worker based in India needs to work from Brazil for a few months, which can be handled generally by an "exceptions" vendor group. This is for those who have a valid business reason to not fit into the existing vendor user groups for a finite period of time. Do not allow these to become permanent exceptions; instead, expect them to be bound by a short expiration period. This exceptions list should be reviewed often—perhaps weekly or monthly, depending on your risk appetite—for any that are on there too long or any that can drop off early due to no longer being needed.

Auditing   The exceptions vendor group being reviewed on a regular basis is a reminder that logging and auditing of vendor user accounts is an important part of the ZT strategy. Log what each account does for access, edit, create, and delete with an appropriate review at regular periods, and validate whether there has been any privilege creep (a third-party user has access to a resource they no longer need to access). It is important to monitor the change log for any vendor user account for improper changes to password, permissions, or settings.

Transaction: Scan All Content for Third-Party Malicious Activity

Scan all content for vendor malicious activity. This requires several processes and tools for complete coverage. Scanning here is focused on user activity and their devices. In this transaction phase, the focus is on malicious activity from a vendor-based user. You can look for bad behavior by a third-party user in a number of ways. Typical in an enterprise is an intrusion detection or prevention system (IDS/IPS), data loss prevention (DLP), security incident and event management (SIEM), and user behavior anomaly detection (UBAD).

IDS/IPS　Leveraging these systems to detect or prevent an intrusion is typically the realm of cybersecurity operations or other technical departments. Getting them tuned to look for intrusions from third parties is relatively easy if the right groups have been set up. Start with a small test group or two, and then build on those until the number of groups is correct for your risk appetite. The system can then be tuned to look for thresholds, depending on the type of IDS/IPS, to set off alarms or shut off access when behavior deviates from what is expected in that third-party user group.

DLP　Most DLP systems are run with desktop agents and can be combined with a number of network flow "traps" to capture any data transiting various modes of transport (email, HTTPS, HTTP, FTP, fixed line [MPLS, VPN], etc.). In many cases, the vendor's equipment may not be in your organization's direct control and so may not have the agents running for that control. However, the data flows can be monitored for data classification missteps, for example, or can leverage a next-generation firewall to be able to decrypt traffic and inspect for violations. There is too much trust in vendor communications, and having that traffic inspected to ensure it meets the vendor's contractual ability to share data of a sensitive classification is crucial to ZT.

SIEM Again, many SIEM systems are leveraged by cyber operations teams that are focused, as a rule, on their internal systems and threats directed at the organization (not so much on third parties). Working with the teams that use these tools, it can be easiest to leverage existing groups already created in the Active Directory (many of these tools can do this task) to look for anomalous behavior. Set thresholds for when activity becomes out of the normal. For example, if the vendor user suddenly triples the amount of data upload, that might be a threshold to look into for any malicious behavior.

UBAD UBAD has been evolving and maturing rapidly, and with user behavior analytics (UBA) it can be leveraged to detect anomalous behavior by a third-party user. Bringing together data science, machine learning, algorithms, and artificial intelligence, these UBA systems can be tuned to look for third-party users who are behaving in ways out of their normal pattern. This takes time to tune, but a baseline can be quickly established based on other similar vendor users. These UBAD solutions collect data from a variety of sources (IAM logs, network logs, transaction logs, etc.) to provide a complete behavior pattern of that third-party user. Users often do the same thing, the same way, day in and out. If that behavior changes in a way that is beyond the normal, they can be tuned to alert or cut off access. This is a bit of an oversimplification of a system that looks at human behavior, which is complex as well. However, UBAD is a key piece of looking for malicious third-party user activity, and more mature programs would benefit from leveraging them around critical, sensitive assets and resources.

Governance   All of the above actions, controls, and policies are required to be part of a governance process. A *governance process* is a series of policies and processes that ensure compliance guidelines that direct actions such as who can access, share, or use sensitive data. This governance should include important steps in how access is granted, monitored (such as access reviews), and revoked properly. The need to have a governance process and program cannot be stressed enough to provide both preventive and detective controls for access.

Zero Trust and Third-Party Users Summary

Implementing ZT for third-party users, broken down into the four categories (identity, device/workload, access, and transaction), allows your ZT team to tackle this important pillar (third-party users) more easily:

- **Identity**: Validate third-party users with strong authentication.
  - Strong authentication and/or multifactor for all third-party access
  - Stronger identity requirements than yours
- **Device/Workload**: Verify third-party user device integrity.
  - 802.1x enforcement on all third-party devices
  - Quarantine process and process to remove
- **Access**: Enforce least-privilege access for third-party users to data and apps.

- Third parties access what they need only while they need it
- Access reviews for third parties with accountability
- **Transaction**: Scan all content for third-party malicious activity and data theft.

  - Any third-party user and their devices must be included in an IDS/IPS
  - Any third-party user and their devices must be included in a SEIM
  - Any third-party user and their devices must be included in DLP
  - Any third-party user and their devices must be included in any UBAD

Zero Trust and Third-Party Applications

Third-party applications are an extremely weak link in most supply chains and third-party cyber risk management organizations. Most organizations are far too trusting of third-party software (this runs from commercial-off-the-shelf [COTS] to APIs) than their own risk appetites allow, and it is viewed as something too tough to tackle. The SolarWinds hack, which had an advanced persistent threat (APT) actor inject malware into that product for download, saw that over-trustworthiness exposed. Solar-Winds is the one most commonly known, but there are hundreds of examples across the world in the last two years where a bad actor has placed malware into an application or code to exploit it on that product and leverage your organization's reliance on that third-party product to get into your network and your data.

Identity: Validate Third-Party Developers, DevOps, and Admins with Strong Auth

You've already read what strong authentication is related to users earlier in this chapter. Because this section focuses on privileged or super-user accounts, though, here the focus is more specific and direct with regard to how to secure these accounts for vendors. *Privileged accounts* are those with elevated rights to perform activities ordinary users are not authorized to perform. That may sound vague but is a common definition. To be more specific, these are the vendor accounts that have the ability to change permissions, delete data, steal data, look at data without rights, and more.

Privileged User Groups As with normal user accounts, creating a group for vendor privileged users is a needed first step. The groups allow their permissions to be centralized and properly managed. First rule of thumb: There should not be many vendors or people in this group. There is no hard rule that says "one privileged user for every 10 users," but best practice is that any single resource requiring administrative access should be less than a handful, in most cases. For vendor users to have privileged accounts, it should be kept to the bare minimum, and always question why it needs to expand. Do not allow normal users this level of access who do not need it. This can happen with a lazy system administrator who does not want to take the time to fine-tune a user's access or find the correct user group.

Multifactor Authentication MFA must be required for all vendor privileged access. Full stop. Only checking one factor (username and password) is not sufficient, given the risk posed by an administrator for applications or other critical resources.

MFA implementation for vendors should use more reliable forms of authentication, such as biometrics or OTPs, to ensure the person is truly authenticated.

Just-in-Time Access   Access for accounts with privilege should be time bound and not unlimited. Again, ZT principles assume a breach and seek to reduce the blast radius. Limiting the amount of time and/or when a privileged third-party user can access is key to reducing this blast radius.

Privileged Access Management   PAM systems are an important factor in successfully implementing ZT because they are key to reducing the risk and blast radius inherent in privileged accounts. Most PAM systems offer the following features:

- Access manager: Stores permissions and privileged user info
- Password vault: Stores the passwords securely
- Session tracker: Tracks privileged sessions once granted
- MFA: Requires MFA for administrators
- Dynamic settings: Allows for granting access for specific periods of time or other settings
- Automation: Automated provisioning and deprovisioning to reduce insider threats
- Logging: Ability to log everything

Tying the Active Directory privileged groups to the PAM system, either digitally with an API or manually entering them, is the key step here to ensure vendor administrative users are being managed in your organization's PAM system. Also note these other key elements. Ensure that administrators are not allowed to share accounts, ever. A user must have only one privileged account. Enforce separation of duties and least privilege. Document the process for approvals of elevated access. Ensure there is a logging review process.

Audit and Logging Logging and auditing of privileged accounts used by vendors should be a much more frequent activity than for normal users (at least once a quarter, in most organizations, if not more often depending on activity and risk appetite). These accounts represent the biggest threat to your secrets and data, so reviewing their use and approvals should be done as often as possible. This is part of your IAM governance process and policies. Who reviews these logs is important because only certain teams will know who is supposed to be an administrator or privileged user. Ensure that the process for this review is clearly documented and that the internal "owner" for the application or resource reviews the privileged user access as required.

Device/Workload: Verify Third-Party Workload Integrity

The validation of workload integrity refers to determining if the application or service meets the security requirements listed for your organization. This section discusses the typical method to do so.

When a new zero-day vulnerability is detected on third-party software deployed in your data center, at a basic level a ZT deployment would be able to make that connection (due to constant scanning and knowing what's on your network) so corrective action can be planned and taken. At this level, the organization has performed scanning and is aware, via a configuration management database (CMDB) or similar system of record (SoR) for resources, of the third-party application. The scanning includes getting intelligence and patching updates via a number of sources that are correlated manually (not ideal, but it depends on the size of your shop) to another software that tracks all this for your organization. Making this connection is the *never trust* part of the ZT concepts. Now your team knows the software cannot be trusted, and because it's been tracked, the team can go get it planned and patched as soon as possible.

A more mature ZT deployment would be able to quarantine the affected resource until it can be patched or modify controls to mitigate the new vulnerability. The quarantining is more mature because it involves a lot more coordination and planning than just finding it. These resources are in motion and in use, so there are other resources (users, servers) utilizing them. To quarantine this third-party application (resource) means depriving those other resources of their access. The downstream effects of a quarantine must be mapped out before the action is taken and a published escalation process that is taken in tandem with cutting off the access to the third-party application. Meanwhile there is a concurrent effort underway to determine what corrective action and/or mitigating controls need to be planned and executed. None of these can be done successfully ad hoc more than once, so it requires not only documentation but also practice via tabletop exercises, to ensure it goes off as planned. And there is the needed postmortem of each tabletop and production incident to learn and improve.

Access: Enforce Least-Privilege Access for Third-Party Workloads Accessing Other Workloads

No different than for end users, it is in many ways more important to use least-privilege access principles for any third-party workloads. This can be anything from a vendor-supplied application and its associated services, an Internet of Things (IoT) device, or an external vendor API accessing something internal to your network. The reason these are more important is because they are often forgotten about once set up by the vendor or whoever installs the software or provides access to the application, device, or service.

First and foremost, never accept a vendor's software internally to run or access your network that requires root or super-user access in any fashion. While I'd prefer not to have to write that last sentence, there are still times when you can hear a vendor say this is what their software "requires" to perform at peak. This is nonsense and is just lazy planning and coding, and a security nightmare. Don't fall for it. Walk away from that vendor.

Okay, now that is out of the way, it's time to ensure that your internal processes are ready to handle a least-privilege access model and ensure the vendor's software, device, or service (or all three) only requires the access it needs. If there is any privileged access, it is vastly preferred if the software can integrate with PAM software to lower the risk of the credentials being stolen. If they cannot, require the privileged access to be reviewed and approved at least every quarter or every three months. These privileged accounts should be monitored and be part of a "special" area in the SIEM team because this is not your software but someone else's running in your house. Remember SolarWinds? We all have trusted externally provided third-party software without question, and this Achilles heel is what the bad actors took advantage of in that case. The real target of the folks behind SolarWinds was not SolarWinds but the three-letter U.S. government agencies' files and some high-value intellectual property at some high-tech firms.

Transaction: Scan All Content for Third-Party Malicious Activity and Data Theft

As content from third parties enters or traverses your organization's network, there must be a view to any unwanted activity or data exfiltration. In addition, there are tools in categories labeled

Vendor Security Ratings that themselves are software-as-a-service (SaaS) applications. These tools can be leveraged to look for malicious activity or potential data theft; this is accomplished with a cyber continuous monitoring program, which is covered at a high level. (You can find coverage of it in greater detail in my first book, *Cybersecurity and Third-Party Risk: Third Party Threat Hunting, Wiley, 2021*.)

As for the initial aspect of security risk, which involves third-party content traversing your network, larger organizations often need to engage in collaboration with multiple internal groups that manage various capabilities: data loss prevention, enterprise data, network security, security operations, and the SIEM team. It could be more or less, and the names of departments vary, but the outcome needs to be the same: Ensure the view of all data traffic and how that data gets analyzed and alerted and then collaborate to plug in vendor names to look for any traffic being sent in the clear (unencrypted) that should not be due to misclassification. When those are discovered, it is often scope creep in a relationship with a vendor or a miss on intake due diligence. However, these are often easy wins that can validate the effort to find these gaps and close them. And this should become a business-as-usual function, meaning the teams are always looking (either real-time or on a scheduled basis) for new unencrypted/unauthorized vendor-to-customer traffic.

Once the vendor traffic has been confirmed as encrypted and there is a process to always check for new violators, the program can become more robust and focus on leveraging the latest firewalls to allow traffic to be decrypted and ensure no data loss is occurring with the vendor traffic. Then add the SIEM tools to look for anomalous behaviors. You must tune these tools over time, but they can help to become more predictive, and when a breach does occur, you'll have a great audit trail to determine a lot of lessons learned.

Zero Trust and Third-Party Applications Summary

Applications are everywhere, and we trust them too much. To address this issue of overtrust when implementing ZT, you must ensure to validate any vendors responsible for application development and administration via strong authentication, such as MFA and PAM. The workload integrity validation is to ensure no anomalous behavior by the application or device as it runs in your network. Enforcing least privilege for applications, services, or devices can be challenging in cases where the developers have not had security at top of mind. However, even when good coding provides good granular access controls, it is often overlooked because they are not users but "system" accounts. Lastly, a lot of vendor traffic likely traverses your organization's network. The old ways of a vendor only connecting via a leased line or with a fileshare still exist (but in limited numbers). Most of the connectivity is going through your network and must be monitored and managed for any malicious activity or data loss. Although applications are ubiquitous and overtrusted, there are ways to enforce a ZT model for third-party applications running in your domain.

Zero Trust and Third-Party Infrastructure

Third-party infrastructure and ZT are often areas overlooked because equipment or hardware is not tracked or gets lost in the onboarding. Examples of third-party infrastructure include networking equipment, servers, laptops, security cameras, IP phones, printers, and any other type of equipment connected to the network. It is a very rare case when your organization is making its own equipment of this type, and it is common to have a vendor solve for these capabilities. However, much like software, many organizations are too trusting of third-party infrastructure in their enterprise. First, many organizations need to ensure they are tracking third-party infrastructure in their own inventory systems (for example, a CMDB). Next, the organization must ensure they are identifying which of these devices in their CMDB are from a third party and/or managed by a third party. Ensure those devices have access only to resources required to perform their capability and scan continually for any malicious activity by any of this third-party infrastructure.

Identity: Validate Third-Party Users with Access to Infrastructure

Third-party users with access to infrastructure are those vendor resources (people) who come onsite to work or connect remotely to work on some infrastructure (networking gear, telecommunications, or physical access controls, for example). The physical access for most organizations can be often overlooked as "already handled" because you have a reception team that checks badges and logs visitors by checking a valid identification card. That may be the case, and congratulations, but what is your policy when these vendors have access to your network and other areas that will provide them access to sensitive data? Visitors who are going to gain access to your network equipment or your security systems should be treated the same way you'd treat a strange contractor who comes to your home: Always accompany them, and although you don't want to watch them to the point of making them uncomfortable, it is okay to observe and ensure they're doing the work as expected and nothing more.

The logical access of third parties to infrastructure is often in the form of a remote session into the infrastructure device. This "session" can be initiated through various means, from virtual desktop to Telnet, Remote Desktop Protocol, and so on. A secure session (communication means) is crucial and should be an industry best practice (for instance, encrypted in transit and requiring a solid access authorization process). Numerous options are available to address this requirement effectively. As these users must be in a third-party user group in the Active Directory to have access, this should be tied to an access approval and review system already in place. Larger organizations can automate this process, while smaller teams can do this manually with a risk-based lens to focus on privileged accounts in particular. Ensure these privileged accounts are tied to your PAM system, if available, to allow for just-in-time, granular access when needed for these vendors.

Another aspect of vendor access control involves out-of-band devices. These devices are used to connect a vendor to a device through a secondary interface separate from the device's primary interface. Often these are modems or an alternate telecommunications device to connect to critical infrastructure in case of an outage on the primary connection. This can also be done with serial console servers at a data center and a remote office to have an alternate path to critical network infrastructure. For example, you can leverage a 5G cell connection to provide secondary access in case of a primary outage. To ensure these are secure, look for next-generation firewalls to be utilized, with a secure provisioning guide from the vendor, have an owner responsible for updating with patches for the connection's hardware, and ensure that vendors log in with MFA.

Device/Workload: Identify All Third-Party Devices (Including IoT)

The number of connected devices in many organizations continues to multiply, and the need to identify them and catalog them is crucial to be able to lower the risk. An ideal way to identify any device on your network, third-party or otherwise is with Network Access Control (NAC), or 802.1x, deployed across your enterprise.

802.1x, or IEEE 802.1x, is an IEEE standard for port-based network access controls. 802.1x requires an authentication server to check whether a user's credentials allow that user access to the network. There can be policies that allow for network access that is granular and can isolate third-party devices on separate VLANs, for example, or place them in a quarantine until validated for other controls. 802.1x provides a device access to the network once authentication has occurred successfully. User identity is determined based on credentials/certificates (sometimes credentials and a certificate are considered MFA). Once the user is confirmed on the RADIUS server, communication can occur via Lightweight Directory Access Protocol (LDAP) or Security Assertion Markup Language (SAML), providing different deployment options.

> 802.1x is not impregnable, and, in particular, the wireless areas are the most vulnerable. Pre-Shared Key (PSK) is for home use and is the push-button option you see on many home-use network devices. Never use PSK in any corporate or protected setting, and frankly you shouldn't use it at home either. It is quite easily broken. Other options such as PEAP MSCHAPv2 (Protected Extensible Authentication Protocol with Microsoft Handshake Authentication Protocol version 2) and EAP-TTLS/PAP (Extensible Authentication Protocol-Tunneled Transport Layer Security / Password Authentication Protocol) have been cracked or are considered too vulnerable. The only current option for security is to use EAP-TLS. Make sure they are using this form of authentication.

If your enterprise has not deployed an 802.1x solution, network discovery may be occurring in other ways, but with fewer preventive measures and more focus on detection. There are numerous ways to do this. Your SIEM team might be responsible for detecting and collecting this data. Your networking team may scan and maintain logs of devices connecting to the network. Alternatively, you might outsource this to a managed service provider. The primary requirement is that all third-party devices connected to your network (whether IoT, networking equipment, cameras, and so on) be registered in a searchable database or SoR.

These devices must also meet a minimum standard for identification and authorization to access the network. For example, they must be 802.1x compliant. This is not a new standard, and any manufacturer should support this important protocol for any device that can potentially connect to a network (wireless or wired). There are a few categories of a device's connection standard for third parties in your organization.

Software-Defined Perimeter 802.1x, or NAC, described earlier, is familiar to many organizations and is an adequate way to tackle some of the policy-based controls in ZT deployments. However, a better solution is a software-defined perimeter (SDP). An *SPD* is a security method to control access to assets based on the identity and forms a "virtual" boundary around resources. The approach essentially "hides" Internet-connected infrastructure (servers, routers, cloud access points) so that external users and hackers cannot see it, whether on-premises or in the cloud. Think of an SPD as a virtual boundary rather than the traditional "old" boundary of firewalls and "hard" network access points.

Encryption All communications and data stored on the devices must be encrypted at rest and in transit. The encryption must be an industry standard and acceptable algorithm. Never accept a vendor who has a proprietary encryption algorithm; those have never worked out well for the vendor nor for the customer because they typically are easily breakable, and no one really knows who has the keys when it is hidden from your scrutiny.

Updates   The products must support automatic updates for at least three years after sale, and those updates must be enabled by default. Updates must also be signed, and the device must only accept digitally signed software. This ensures that once installed and turned on, no matter how complacent the service technicians may be, it will be ready to securely accept needed security updates in a timely fashion. A word of caution on automatic updates: Always consider the risk versus reward (think Solar-Winds and how automatic updates in that case caused many to get the compromised code). If the code is digitally signed and there is an urgent need to perform the automatic updates due to criticality of the software, it should be considered carefully.

Enforce Strong Passwords   The product must force a password change by default for first-time use and have password complexity and length requirements to meet your own minimum standards. One suggestion is requiring a minimum of 15 characters, with changes permissible only once a year. There must be no backdoors in the system at all, and this should be in any terms and conditions clauses with these vendors. Any passwords stored on the system must be encrypted.

Vulnerability and Secure Development Management   The third party must have a vulnerability management system in place for reporting and updating them as they become known to the vendor. The vendor should have a bug bounty program and/ or a number to report suspected vulnerabilities. In addition, regardless of if this is a piece of hardware (camera, network hardware) or software (third-party application or workload), the vendor must have a secure development program.

Logging and Monitoring   The vendor's device or workload must allow logs to be forwarded to a log server of the customer's choice. This enables the SIEM teams or other monitoring teams to inform your team of any anomalies or behavior of note with the device. If the device supports Simple Network Management Protocol (SNMP), it must support SNMPv3 (the most secure deployment of this protocol).

Access: Enforce Least-Privilege Access Segmentation for Third-Party Infrastructure

Least-privilege access is fundamental to a ZT strategy, and is particularly critical to third-party infrastructure (devices and workloads) within your organization. After you have identified and verified all third-party devices and infrastructure on your network (as in the previous steps), you can most likely categorize them based on use case. For example, a medium-size company with international teams might have the following:

- Security devices: Security cameras, locked doors, motion sensors
- Building controls: Heating/cooling, fire control systems
- Network: Telecom and related hardware
- Collaboration equipment: Big-screen displays and video-conferencing hardware

Each device type presents its own unique sort of security challenge, but the choice becomes whether to create a separate

VLAN for each or run a single VLAN isolated for just third-party devices. This depends on your risk appetite. Considering the four types listed above, however, it is recommended to isolate the security and building controls in a separate VLAN (because of what they can touch and control).

Another way to isolate or segment a third-party device or workload is to create a demilitarized zone (DMZ) or enclave. The enclave or DMZ offers a layer of protection from a rogue device, potentially, by ensuring the area only allows for traffic permitted by design. For example, if you have a vendor device that is only supposed to communicate out of port 83 (making this up), then the enclave will only allow for that type of traffic on that port. Further, placing the DMZ behind a next-generation firewall can provide a layer of transparency to the traffic in and out for more security on the monitoring side.

Transaction: Scan All Content Within the Infra for Third-Party Malicious Activity and Data Theft

As transactions are occurring, meaning activity with third-party content within your network, you must have continuous scanning and monitoring in place through both a SIEM and a DLP system. Most likely, your SIEM and DLP teams, or equivalent in smaller teams, are aware of these transactions but may not know the risk or owner. Linking your inventory of known third-parties and the scanning of the devices done, and then having the SIEM team be on the lookout for anomalous behavior or the CLP team knowing what level of data is allowed to be transferred to a vendor, is the critical step to complete.

Zero Trust and Third-Party Infrastructure Summary

The last row in our OSI model can be a challenge in some organizations because the infrastructure pieces are the least cataloged and managed. Third-party devices are often overlooked because the vendor is "done" in many ways: They sold you the product. Your own organization may find it difficult to catalog them because they are not picked by your access management team, and there can be thousands of variations of device types. However, setting minimum standards for your organization as to what these devices should support for security drastically lowers your risk and enables a comprehensive ZT strategy that seeks to identify devices, ensure those devices can support least-privilege access, and enable scanning for malicious activity or data loss activities.

3

Zero Trust and Fourth-Party Cloud (SaaS)

Many solutions that vendors offer today are cloud-based software offerings, known as software-as-a-service (SaaS). Most often, these SaaS solutions run on a cloud service provider (CSP) such as Amazon Web Services, Microsoft Azure, or Google Cloud. Ensuring that the vendor is practicing a zero trust (ZT) journey with regard to how they've deployed a SaaS solution to your organization can be challenging because the CSP is a fourth party. Therefore, there is no ability for your ZT team to engage directly with AWS or Azure or Google. However, there are ways to leverage guidance from these CSPs and utilize the evidence they produce to determine whether the vendor is using ZT practices with their cloud vendor.

As this chapter covers each of the CSPs, you'll learn how each of the big three providers describes the technologies used in their space for ZT. While technologies are not themselves ZT, we do need to know if the vendor has deployed the specific technologies associated with successful ZT. The next step is to examine whether the vendor has policies and processes to enforce ZT principles, such as least privilege or microsegmentation. Each CSP uses different terminology to describe their solutions for technologies, such as least-privilege access or microsegmentation. After noting the names of these being used or available for use by the vendor in their SaaS solution, the discussion turns to testing if they are using these solutions in a ZT approach.

Cloud Service Providers and Zero Trust

The big three CSPs all describe how to implement ZT in their cloud environments. Keep in mind that this is for their direct customers, in this case, your vendor, who is leveraging these controls to better the security of the product you consume. This discussion focuses on SaaS deployments because that is the overwhelming use case for most customers. As you read through the big three CSPs how-to guides here, keep in mind that the principles and strategy are the same. The biggest difference is how the CSPs name their products within their own systems. For the purposes of this book, it is not expected for you to be an expert on the offerings from the CSPs. Instead, the goal here is to provide enough information so that you can query your vendors that leverage a CSP to deliver a SaaS solution, where the vendor is on their ZT journey.

Zero Trust in Amazon Web Services

Amazon Web Services (AWS) has done an excellent job at providing its customers with guidance on how to implement ZT on their deployments inside AWS. To better understand how zero trust is implemented in the SaaS solution provided by your vendor, you should inquire about their specific implementation. AWS offers both identity-centric and network-centric tools that complement each other to achieve ZT. Identity-centric tools, such as AWS SigV4 request-signing process, are used for secure interaction between AWS API endpoints and ensure fine-grained access controls. Network-centric controls in AWS include Amazon Virtual Private Cloud (Amazon VPC), security groups, AWS PrivateLink, and VPC endpoints. All are used to keep unneeded traffic out of the network and work with the identity-centric controls to provide guardrails for operations.

A prime example of effective ZT implementation in AWS focuses on lowering the risk to lateral communications within the network. Machine-to-machine communications should be controlled and allowed only when required. Ensuring this interconnectivity is authorized lowers the surface area a hacker can gain access to, and thus sensitive data is better protected. A vendor using AWS should be using security groups as part of an Amazon EC2 deployment to provide very dynamic, software-defined network perimeters for both north-south and east-west network traffic. These security group assignments should be dynamic and automatic as resources are onboarded and offboarded. Rules in one security group can be referenced in another security group by an ID; this can be done within the same Amazon VPC or across larger networks in the same, or different,

AWS regions. This allows for the scale and redundancy across the AWS network with the ZT granularity on network access controls.

AWS PrivateLink provides private connectivity between Amazon VPCs, supported AWS services, and your vendor's on-premises networks without exposing the traffic to the public. A vendor can leverage this PrivateLink to expose a narrow one-way gateway between two VPCs, with very granular identity-based controls that determine who gains access to the link and where the traffic can go. Thousands of AWS customers use PrivateLink to provide secure, private access to their SaaS solutions if required. The last example of secure network communications in AWS is the Amazon API Gateway service, which allows these crucial (but risky) software interfaces to be available securely on the open Internet. The API Gateway service provides distributed denial-of-service (DDoS) protection, rate limiting, and AWS Identity and Access Management (IAM) support for authorization options. When a vendor successfully leverages AWS IAM along with the API Gateway service, they will have API calls that sign their requests using AWS credentials, which allow AWS IAM to authenticate and authorize every single call to their API. All these calls are secured with Transport Layer Security (TLS) encryption and identity-centric and network-centric controls.

Amazon Web Services offers Amazon Workspaces, which is their named version of a virtual desktop, to allow for securing the end device (the virtual desktop) to the granularity required by you as the ultimate customer in this relationship. If the product offered is an application-as-a-service, the Amazon AppStream product is aligned with the ZT security tooling required. For SaaS offerings that are on a mobile device that requires mobile device management (MDM), Amazon WorkLink is the solution offered because it provides a way to send data to the mobile phone without data being stored on the device.

Lastly, inquire if your vendor is going to be moving the application into the AWS cloud, or whether they plan to connect their internal SaaS (at the third-party's own data center, not in an AWS data center) to their customers (your organization, in this case). While most vendors choose to convert and host their applications completely within the AWS cloud, implementing the security controls mentioned earlier for their ZT journey, you should inquire whether the third party is planning to connect their own internal SaaS to AWS Cloud. You want to know whether they are leveraging items such as AWS Shield, AWS Web Application Firewall (WAF), and Application Load Balancer with OpenID Connect authentication. If so, such use indicates that they are focused on a ZT approach.

Once you've determined the vendor is using the expected technologies in AWS, you next want to check whether they are implementing ZT processes and architecture (with the AWS tools) to effectively implement ZT.

Zero Trust in Azure

Azure provides several guides for how to implement ZT, and some are not aligned to what we'd want to evaluate for a third party's SaaS application. Because Microsoft provides on-prem software and infrastructure, there are guides about ZT for similar environments (or how your own team can deploy Microsoft 365 with a ZT plan). This discussion, however, focuses on how to apply ZT principles to Azure infrastructure. This how-to guide provides what a typical vendor would do and the products they'd use to implement ZT on a SaaS offering. Azure breaks down the design and implementation into three security principles for ZT:

- Verify explicitly.
- Use least-privilege access.
- Assume breach.

As explained by Microsoft, adopting a ZT mindset requires that you assume breach, never trust, and always verify. This mindset should then lead to changes in the cloud infrastructure, deployment strategies, and implementation methods. There are reference architectures provided on Azure for common deployments for customers to reuse/edit. The guidance is broken down into larger architectural areas:

- Azure storage services
- Virtual machines
- Spoke VNets
- Hub VNets

The extent to which the vendor has incorporated various types of products to provide the SaaS application determines how effectively they've implemented a ZT approach. Here are some of the tools and technologies a vendor would deploy and what they are used for:

- Azure subscription: This is a base requirement to host something at Azure.
- Microsoft Defender for Cloud and Azure Monitor: This tool is their offering for extended detection and response solution.
- Storage resource group: Just like it sounds, this is where storage accounts and resources are contained and provides for granular access control.

- Virtual machines resource group: Virtual machines should be contained in one resource group and a virtual machine (VM) for each type of workload type (front end, application, and data) to allow for different resource groups to have improved access control isolation.

- Spoke-and-hub VNet resource groups: Network and resources for each of VNets must be isolated within dedicated resource groups. This isolation improves separation of duties and least privilege. Or the vendor could organize the components with all network resources in a single resource group and security resources in a separate resource group.

There are in-depth articles on how to implement ZT in each of the four architectural areas. The following sections discuss the high-level steps the vendor must take to implement Azure tools correctly to match their ZT goals.

Zero Trust in Azure Storage   Enabling ZT in Azure Storage involves focusing on key aspects such as encrypting the data, implementing least-privilege access controls, utilizing microsegmentation, and leveraging Azure Defender for Storage:

- **Protect data in transit, at rest, and in use:** This is accomplished by encryption in transit. The vendor should prevent anonymous public read access and not allow for shared key authorization. Enforcement of a minimum required version of TLS (should be nothing lower than 1.2) is required, and some limitation of the scope of copy operations for storage accounts should be enabled. Storage is automatically encrypted at AES-256.

- **Verify users and control access using least privilege:** Azure recommends that the vendor use Azure Active

Directory to manage storage account access, with the goal of allowing the vendor to granularly define access based on the role (a role-based access control [RBAC]-based model) and leveraging OAuth 2.0. Further, they can align the granular access with their conditional access policy. Another way for a vendor to manage time-bound limits on access is via shared access signature (SAS) user resource identifiers (URIs). Ensure the vendors follow the best practices from Azure when using SAS:

- Always use HTTPS.
- Have a revocation plan.
- Configure an expiration policy for any SAS.
- Validate permissions.
- Prefer the use of user delegation SAS, which is signed with Azure AD credentials.

- **Separate sensitive data or processes using microsegmentation:** There are three main tasks listed for this:
  - Prevent public access, create network segmentation using private endpoints and private links.
  - Use Azure Private Link.
  - Prevent public access to data sources using service end points.

- **Defender for Storage must be used for auto threat detection and protection:** Clear guidance is provided on the configuration and functionality of this system. For inquiring with the vendor, focus on whether they deployed the tool and whether they have a process to track and resolve any issues found.

Zero Trust on Azure Virtual Machines The instruction for implementing ZT in Azure VMs covers the entire logical architecture, down to the data and application layer within each VM:

- All VMs must have logical isolation
- RBACs
- VM boot components secured
- Allow for customer-managed keys and double encryption
- All applications on VMs must be controlled
- Secure access controls
- Secure maintenance of VMs
- Advanced threat detection and protections enabled

Most of these steps are as described and do not need further instruction. They serve as a checklist for vendors to confirm whether they've taken each of these steps when using VMs in their product.

Zero Trust on an Azure Spoke VNet Implementing ZT on an Azure spoke VNet includes these steps:

- Azure Active Directory RBAC or use custom rules for networking resources
- Infrastructure in its own resource group
- Each subnet has its own network security group
- Each VM role has an application security group
- Ensure secure access for VNet and applications
- Advanced threat detection and protection enabled

Again, most of these are steps that the vendor should follow when using the spoke VNet product in Azure when ZT is a goal.

Zero Trust on an Azure Hub VNet Implementing ZT on an Azure hub VNet includes these steps:

- Deploy and secure Azure Firewall Premium
- Azure DDoS Protection Standard
- Configure network gateway routing to the firewall
- Configure threat protection for the hub VNet

If the vendor chooses to deploy a hub VNet solution, usually involving a bastion or demilitarized zone (DMZ) with firewalls, it is crucial to consider the logical location of these types of devices (because DMZ/bastion are not safe zones by definition). Therefore, it is vital to ensure that the vendor followed the steps to secure this space.

Zero Trust in Azure Summary Azure provides detailed road-maps and steps for a vendor to enable a ZT strategy for nearly every deployment, including a SaaS product to you as a customer. The two steps you want to complete to assess the vendor's implementation of ZT is first knowing the terminology and tools they offer the vendor and then validating that the vendor has effective processes and policies in place and practice.

Zero Trust in Google Cloud

Google was an early and ardent adopter of ZT security due to an attack on their own network and a desire to reduce the risk of this happening again. They created BeyondCorp as their solution for this strategy. The tools Google brings to bear in this space are listed here, along with their recommendations as to how they should be implemented to succeed in ZT. To ensure vendor compliance with ZT principles in Google Cloud, you want to confirm that they have designated the SaaS applications they host as protected resources. In addition, they should have the web application operating behind a load balancer on Google Cloud, and have established access limits and principles that align with ZT principles.

Identity-Aware Proxy By using Identity-Aware Proxy (IAP) in Google Cloud, the vendor can establish centralized identity awareness for applications, resources, and workloads accessed via HTTPS and TCP. This allows the vendor to control access for each application, resource, or workload rather than having to use a network layer firewall. Google Cloud can host a vendor's on-premises SaaS application as if it is in their cloud, but you always want to be sure to ask whether it just within Google Cloud (and not elsewhere). Google provides multiple guides on how to secure a SaaS application based on type:

- **Application engines:** These are where most of the SaaS applications that you would consume from a vendor sit. If the vendor uses one of these types, they should have used this guide or be able to speak to their implementation of IAP. Focus on the tool deployment first, and then ensure their implementation aligns with your expectations for ZT.

- **Compute engine applications**: These are defined as a customizable service that allows you to create and run VMs.

If the vendor leverages this type of product for your consumption, ensure they have followed this runbook by Google's team.

- **Google Kubernetes Engine (KGE):** These are defined as a managed environment for scaling containers within the Google Cloud. Typically, this would not be something you'd see as a customer. However, it might be how the vendor is managing multiple containerized applications for multiple customers, including your organization.

Access Context Manager   Once the work has been done to secure their SaaS applications and resources in IAP, the next step the vendor takes is to set access policies with access levels. The Access Context Manager tool enables the vendor to limit access based on at least five attributes:

- **IP subnetworks:** This allows the vendor to limit by blocking by IP address and port.
- **Regions:** Based on IP range region attribute, the vendor can limit access by geography.
- **Access level dependency:** This ensures the access request meets at least one or more criteria for access.
- **Principles:** This confirms whether a request is coming from a specific user or service account.
- **Device policy:** This allows for a device-level policy, and with Mobile Device Management (MDM) enabled can be for mobile devices.

At this point, the vendor would create an access level on their own or follow Google's access level guide. The vendor would add an IAM condition on the IAP role to provide access to the resources (your SaaS application) and that enables access levels. At this point, once access levels are applied, Google pronounces the application as secured with BeyondCorp Enterprise.

Zero Trust in Google Cloud Summary   For vendors who provide you a SaaS application in Google Cloud, the tools and steps are very clearly laid out by Google itself. There are two major tools to leverage: Identity-Aware Proxy and Access Context Manager. The remaining aspects involve the vendor's implementation of these tools, following the guidelines set by Google, and ensuring adherence to the process for verifying whether the application is truly protected by BeyondCorp Enterprise.

Vendors and Zero Trust Strategy

Once an organization has embarked on their ZT journey by lowering TPR, that organization must deal with an additional area of risk reduction: determining whether the organization's vendors are pursuing their own ZT strategy. This should be a risk-based approach because both your time and resources are going to be spent investigating where your vendors are in their journey. Therefore, it should be focused on third parties that have a significant impact on your organization. You want to carefully consider your approach to this strategy before asking any of your third parties about a ZT program.

Zero Trust at Third Parties as a Requirement

This book deals with how to have your own ZT journey for third parties at your organization. However, one question increasingly asked by customers of their vendors is this: "Are you on a zero trust journey?" ZT is something that all organizations should be deploying, and it is a great question to ask your third parties, particularly the higher-risk vendors in your portfolio. Because ZT is a journey that never really completes, like security, the question of your vendor's journey is more nuanced that a yes/no question and answer. What does it look like to ask this question, and what answers should a vendor provide to enable you to gauge where they are on their journey?

A Starter Zero Trust Security Assessment

First, simply ask the vendor if they are implementing ZT at their firm. Because ZT is a journey or a strategy and not simply a tool or technology, the assessment of their progress will require some engagement and question-and-answer sessions. If the answer is no, they have not begun, or that they just have a roadmap for ZT, the discussion will most likely focus on when they plan to, if ever, implement ZT. If they have begun or are in full swing of implementing it, you want to ask some questions to establish where they are in the overall process:

- Do they have a ZT architecture documented?
- Do they have a ZT team or employees whose main job is to implement it?
  - It should have one or more of the following three areas:
    - Application and data security
    - Network/infrastructure security
    - User and device security
- What area (of the three above) are they focusing on for ZT?
- Have they begun or completed assessing the environment?
  - Where are the current security controls?
  - Are they implementing dynamic, granular trust frame works?
  - Is there a strategy as to which areas they are protecting versus less risky?
- What technologies are they deploying to perform some of the key functions of ZT (microsegmentation, session management, privileged access management, and other capabilities)?

- What is their overall roadmap for ZT deployment?
  - Are they in an early proof-of-concept phase or have they already deployed around their crown jewels and are now focused on later deployments?
- Are they in a monitor mode for any current ZT deployments?
  - Can you validate the monitor mode and feedback loops?

To evaluate their performance, you want to focus your assessment on the following three key areas:

- **ZT for Users**
  - Do they have MFA implemented for access by privileged users, at a minimum? Ideally, they would also have this implemented for any users' access as well.
  - Are they leveraging a PAM system to manage privileged access by administrators?
  - Ask them to demonstrate how they have implemented more strict authentication methods for users.
  - Have they implemented any biometrics for user access?
  - Is there a single IAM system deployed to manage authentication across multiple internal and cloud systems?
  - Is device certification implemented? This is often deployed with 802.1x as a way for systems to be checked prior to accessing the network for patching or malware issues.
  - How effectively do their access policies adapt to incorporate context clues, geolocation, device security posture, and enterprise security policies?
  - Have they planned for just-in-time access controls?
  - What type of governance programs are in place to support user access reviews, and what data regulations are they required to follow?

- **ZT for Applications**
  - Do they have a data classification process documented and implemented? Classification is key to understanding which areas and resources need protecting.
  - Data loss prevention (DLP) tools and processes must be deployed to be able to identify if data exfiltration is taking place.
  - How are they securing the development of software, and are they following a secure development lifecycle?
  - Is there a way they are tracking open source software in their enterprise?
  - Microservices must be authenticated and authorized properly.
  - Containers must be secured using automated deployment, orchestration, tracking, launching, and shutting down of containers.
  - APIs require secure development and deployment as well. Ask how the vendor is approaching this control space.
  - Are they securing application identities (e.g., service accounts) in PAM solutions?
  - How are they managing ephemeral identities?

- **ZT for Infrastructure**
  - Network encryption and secure routing must be deployed. Just because network traffic is internal doesn't mean it should be in the clear.
  - Microsegmentation is a key element of ZT. Data flows must be approved based on user and type of resource, not by port, IP address, and type of traffic.
  - Have they implemented a stateful session management where sessions are managed individually, following them by current state of the connection?

- Are they leveraging any software-defined wide-area network (WAN), secure access service engine (SASE), and/or a cloud access security broker (CASB) to better manage the traffic flows?
- What kind of packet inspection are they doing?

These are just a few of the questions by area that can be leveraged to determine where a vendor is on their ZT journey and help you determine whether they have a well-defined strategy. You should focus on higher-risk vendors when conducting these types of inquiries, as a risk-based approach would imply. Determining whether a vendor has ZT deployed can be time-consuming, given the complexities and variation of deployment strategies.

A Zero Trust Maturity Assessment

Earlier in this book, you read about the importance of a ZT strategy and how it applies to interactions with third-party vendors. Now, it's important to consider the questions of who, what, when, and where to ask these vendors. The who question has a risk-based answer, meaning that the best approach is to focus on higher-risk vendors when you're going to invest this level of time and detail. Best practice is to focus on, at a minimum, those vendors your organization labels as systemically critical for operations. A vendor that your organization cannot run successfully without is one that by definition is one to spend more time with to ensure they are safe and stable. After you have established the universe of who will get this attention, you need to develop a way to determine what specifically you will ask.

The question of what to ask a vendor to determine their ZT strategy is not a checklist. Because it is not a technology or a solution, there needs to be some questions that determine if they have a ZT strategy at all and where they are in the journey. Leveraging the Cybersecurity and Infrastructure Security Vendor (CISA) Zero Trust Maturity Model (April, 2023) v 2.0, along with our ZT and TPR OSI model, we can break down the assessment into four maturity levels:

- **Traditional:** Manual configurations of lifecycles; static security policies; solutions focused within the pillar but very little across pillars; inflexible policy enforcement; manual incident response and mitigations.

- **Initial:** Automation is begun for attribute assignment and configuration of lifecycles, policy decisions, and enforcement; initial solutions integrate with external systems and some least privilege after provisioning, with aggregated visibility for internal systems.

- **Advanced:** Some communications across pillars; central visibility and central identity controls; policy enforcement that crosses pillars; some incident response where predefined; some least-privileged changes based on posture of devices/users/apps.

- **Optimal:** Fully automated from end to end of assets and resources; policies are dynamic and align with open standards for cross-pillar communications and visibility.

CISA breaks segments ZT into five pillars: Identity, Device, Network/Equipment, Application Workload, and Data. These pillars are similar to our OSI model and are a great guide for you to ask where your vendor is in terms of their ZT maturity.

Following is the table translated from the CISA whitepaper with level of maturity on the rows: Traditional, Advanced, and Optimal. The columns are the five ZT pillars. As you go down the rows, the sophistication and maturity of the ZT program is given some high-level bullets.

	Identity	Device	Network/Environment	Application/Workload	Data
Traditional	• Password or MFA • Risk Assessment limited	• Compliance visibility limited • Manual inventory	• Little or no segmentation • Minimal encryption on traffic	• Access is local • Minimal workflow integration • Minimal cloud access	• Limited inventory • Static controls • Unencrypted
Initial	• MFA with passwords • Self-managed and hosted identity stores	• All physical assets tracked • Limited device-access controls	• Initial isolation of critical workloads • Dynamic configurations • More encryption	• Some mission-critical workflows integrated • Static and dynamic security testing	• Limited automation • Begin to implement strategy for data categorization
Advanced	• MFA • Some federation for cloud and on-prem	• Compliance enforced • Data access provided with first-access scan	• Define ingress/egress • Analytics are basic	• Central auth for access • Basic integration for app workflow	• Least privilege controls • Data stored in cloud encrypted
Optimal	• Continuous validation • Real-time ML analysis	• Continual device monitor and validation • Data access with real-time analytics	• Fully distributed ingress/egress • ML-based threat protection • All traffic encrypted	• Continual access authorization • Full integration into app workflow	• Dynamic support • All data encrypted

```
www.cisa.gov/sites/default/files/2023-04/
zero_trust_maturity_model_v2_508.pdf
```
As you move from left to right on each maturity level (Traditional, Advanced, and Optimal), the governance, automation, and orchestration goes across the columns of the five pillars.

Pillar 1: Identity　How the vendor is performing the following functions and at what level will help you grade or determine maturity level. Identity is a critical part of ZT. The more the vendor demonstrates automation and continuous assessments with MFA in all locations, the more mature their program.

Function	Traditional	Initial	Advanced	Optimal
Authentication	Vendor authenticates identity using passwords or MFA.	Vendor authenticates identity using MFA, with one factor being a password.	Vendor authenticates identity using MFA.	Vendor continuously validates identity, not just at initial access.
Identity Stores	Vendor uses on-prem identity stores.	Vendor has a combo of self-managed identity stores and hosted.	Vendor federates some with cloud and on-prem.	Vendor has global identity awareness for both cloud and on-prem.
Risk Assessment	Vendor makes limited determinations for identity risk.	Vendor determines identity risk manually.	Vendor determines identity risk with simple or static rules.	Vendor analyzes user behavior with ML and ongoing risk identification.
Access Management	Vendor provisions permanent access with periodic reviews.	Vendor authorizes access with expiration and auto-mated reviews.	Vendor authorizes need-based, session-based access.	Vendor automates just-in-time and just-enough access.
Visibility and Analytics Capability	Vendor segment user activity based upon basic and static attributes.	Vendor collects user and entity activity logs and performs routine manual analysis and some automated analysis, with limited correlation between log types.	Vendor can aggregate user activity with basic attributes, then analyze and report.	Vendor has central user visibility with user and entity behavior analytics (UEBA).

Function	Traditional	Initial	Advanced	Optimal
Automation and Orchestration Capability	Vendor has manual process for administration and orchestration of identity and credentials.	Vendor manually orchestrates privileged and external identities and automates orchestration of non-privileged users and of self-managed entities.	Vendor uses some basic automation orchestration to federate identity and permit admin across stores.	Vendor has fully orchestrated the identity lifecycle with dynamic user profiling, identity, group membership, and JIT access controls.
Governance Capability	Vendor manually audits process using static technical enforcement of credential policies.	Vendor defines and begins implementing identity policies for enterprise-wide enforcement, with minimal automation and manual updates.	Vendor employs a policy-based auto access revocation. No shared accounts.	Vendor has fully automated technical enforcement of policies and updates policies to reflect new orchestration choices.

Pillar 2: Device Use the following table to determine where the vendor is in terms of their device ZT maturity. As the vendor automates device discovery and improves security posture evaluation, their overall maturity scores increase.

Function	Traditional	Initial	Advanced	Optimal
Policy Enforcement & Compliance Monitoring	Vendor has limited, if any, visibility (i.e., ability to inspect device behavior) into device compliance, with few methods of enforcing policies or managing software, configurations, or vulnerabilities.	Vendor receives self-reported device characteristics (e.g., keys, tokens, users, etc., on the device) but has limited enforcement mechanisms. Vendor has a preliminary, basic process in place to approve software use and push updates and configuration changes to devices.	Vendor has verified insights (i.e., an administrator can inspect and verify the data on device) on initial access to device and enforces compliance for most devices and virtual assets. Vendor uses automated methods to manage devices and virtual assets, approve software, and identify vulnerabilities and install patches.	Vendor continuously verifies insights and enforces compliance throughout the lifetime of devices and virtual assets. Vendor integrates device, software, configuration, and vulnerability management across all vendor environments, including for virtual assets.
Asset & Supply Chain Risk Management	Vendor does not track physical or virtual assets in an enterprise-wide or cross-vendor manner and manages its own supply chain acquisition of devices and services in ad hoc fashion with a limited view of enterprise risks.	Vendor tracks all physical and some virtual assets and manages supply chain risks by establishing policies and control baselines according to federal recommendations using a robust framework.	Vendor begins to develop a comprehensive enterprise view of physical and virtual assets via automated processes that can function across multiple vendors to verify acquisitions, track development cycles, and provide third-party assessments.	Vendor has a comprehensive, at- or near- real-time view of all assets across vendors and service providers, automates its supply chain risk management as applicable, builds operations that tolerate supply chain failures, and incorporates best practices.
Device Threat Protection	Vendor manually deploys threat protection capabilities to some devices.	Vendor has some automated processes for deploying and updating threat protection capabilities to devices and to virtual assets with limited policy enforcement and compliance monitoring integration.	Vendor begins to consolidate threat protection capabilities to centralized solutions for devices and virtual assets and integrates most of these capabilities with policy enforcement and compliance monitoring.	Vendor has a centralized threat protection security solution(s) deployed with advanced capabilities for all devices and virtual assets and a unified approach for device threat protection, policy enforcement, and compliance monitoring.

Resource Access	Vendor data access not dependent on visibility into device.	Vendor requires some devices or virtual assets to report characteristics and then use this information to approve resource access.	Vendor data access does first-access device posture.	Vendor's access to data is performed in real-time device posture.
Visibility and Analytics Capability	Vendor manually inspects labels and periodic network detection and reporting.	Vendor uses digital identifiers (e.g., interface addresses, digital tags) alongside a manual inventory and endpoint monitoring of devices when available. Some vendor devices and virtual assets are under automated analysis (e.g., software-based scanning) for anomaly detection based on risk.	Noncompliance devices are isolated with automation for remaining devices.	Vendor has a continually running device posture assessments and decisioning.
Automation and Orchestration Capability	Vendor manually provisions devices.	Vendor begins to use tools and scripts to automate the process of provisioning, configuration, registration, and/or deprovisioning for devices and virtual assets.	Vendor has automated provisioning.	Vendor has a CI/CD approach to device capacity for dynamic scaling.
Governance Capability	Vendor manually defines and enforces policy.	Vendor sets and enforces policies for the procurement of new devices, the lifecycle of nontraditional computing devices and virtual assets, and for regularly conducting monitoring and scanning of devices.	Vendor minimizes legacy unsupported devices that cannot be automated.	Vendor devices allow data access that is automated and continual.

Pillar 3: Network/Environment The following table describes maturity focused on network and environment. As the vendor increases automation and segmentation, their maturity will increase.

Function	Traditional	Initial	Advanced	Optimal
Network Segmentation	Vendor has little or no segmentation.	Vendor begins to deploy network architecture with the isolation of critical workloads, constraining connectivity to least function principles, and a transition toward service-specific interconnection.	Vendor has some microsegmentation and ingress/egress micro-perimeters.	Vendor has fully distributed ingress/egress micro-perimeters and segmentation of their network.
Network Traffic Management	Vendor manually implements static network rules and configurations to manage traffic at service provisioning, with limited monitoring capabilities.	Vendor establishes application profiles with distinct traffic management features and begins to map all applications to these profiles.	Vendor implements dynamic network rules and configurations for resource optimization that are periodically adapted based upon automated risk-aware.	Vendor implements dynamic network rules and configurations that continuously evolve to meet application profile needs and reprioritize applications.
Traffic Encryption	Vendor encrypts minimal internal/external traffic.	Vendor begins to encrypt all traffic to internal applications, to prefer encryption for traffic to external applications, to formalize key management policies, and to secure server/service encryption keys.	Vendor encrypts all traffic to internal and some external.	Vendor encrypts all traffic to all locations.
Network Resilience	Vendor configures network capabilities on a case-by-case basis to only match individual application availability demands with limited resilience mechanisms for workloads not deemed mission critical.	Vendor begins to configure network capabilities to manage availability demands for additional applications and expand resilience mechanisms for workloads not deemed mission critical.	Vendor has configured network capabilities to dynamically manage the availability demands and resilience mechanisms for the majority of their applications.	Vendor integrates holistic delivery and awareness in adapting to changes in availability demands for all workloads and provides proportionate resilience.

Function	Traditional	Initial	Advanced	Optimal
Visibility and Analytics Capability	Vendor provides views at perimeter centrally aggregated and analyzed.	Vendor employs network monitoring capabilities based on known indicators of compromise (including network enumeration) to develop situational awareness in each environment, and begins to correlate telemetry across traffic types and environments for analysis and threat hunting activities.	Vendor has multiple sensor sets and positions that are integrated with manual policies for alerts and triggers.	Vendor has automated alerts and triggers that are integrated across multiple sensors and locations.
Automation and Orchestration Capability	Vendor has a manual initiated network and environment changes.	Vendor begins using automated methods to manage the configuration and resource lifecycle for some vendor networks or environments and ensures that all resources have a defined lifetime based on policies and telemetry.	Vendor uses automatic workflows to initiate network changes manually.	Vendor uses infra-as-code with continual automation using CI/CD models.
Governance Capability	Vendor relies on manual policies to identify issues.	Vendor defines and begins to implement policies tailored to individual network segments and resources while also inheriting corporate-wide rules as appropriate.	Vendor relies on manual policies to identify issues but has triggers and alerts for manual remediation defined.	Vendor has fully automated discovery, dynamic authorization, and remediation of issues.

Pillar 4: Application/Workload Application ZT maturity focuses on going from manual and static methodology to centralized, automatic, real-time activities around ZT.

Function	Traditional	Initial	Advanced	Optimal
Application Access	Vendor application access is mainly on local auth and static attributes.	Vendor begins to implement authorizing access capabilities to applications that incorporate contextual information (e.g., identity, device compliance, and/or other attributes) per request with expiration.	Vendor access to apps mainly central authentication, authorization, monitoring, and their attributes.	Vendor continually authorizes access to apps with integrated real-time risk analytics.
Application Threat Protections	Vendor's threat protections has minimal integration with apps and only uses known threat patterns.	Vendor integrates threat protections into mission-critical application workflows, applying protections against known threats and some application-specific threats.	Vendor has integrated threat protections in app workflows, with known threats protected.	Vendor has integrated application workflows with threats updated real time and anomalous behavior.
Accessible Applications	Vendor has some critical cloud applications directly accessible over the Internet; all others via VPN only.	Vendor makes some of their applicable mission-critical applications available over open public networks to authorized users via brokered connections.	Vendor has all cloud and on-prem apps accessible directly over the Internet; all others via VPN only.	Vendor has migrated all applications to be accessible over the Internet.
Secure Applications Development and Deployment Workflow	Vendor has ad hoc development, testing, and production environments with non-robust code deployment mechanisms.	Vendor provides infrastructure for development, testing, and production environments (including automation) with formal code deployment mechanisms through CI/CD pipelines and requisite access controls in support of least privilege principles.	Vendor uses distinct and coordinated teams for development, security, and operations while removing developer access to production environment for code deployment.	Vendor leverages immutable workloads where feasible, only allowing changes to take effect through redeployment, and removes administrator access to deployment environments in favor of automated processes for code deployment.

Application Security Testing	Vendor does security testing before deployment, mostly via static and manual testing.	Vendor begins to use static and dynamic (i.e., application is executing) testing methods to perform security testing, including manual expert analysis, prior to application deployment.	Vendor has integrated app security testing in dev and deployment processes and uses dynamic testing.	Vendor fully integrated app security testing in dev and deployment along with automated testing of production apps.
Visibility and Analytics Capability	Vendor has app health and security monitors isolated from external systems.	Vendor begins to automate application profile (e.g., state, health, and performance) and security monitoring for improved log collection, aggregation, and analytics.	Vendor has app health and security monitors context-related to external systems.	Vendor continually and dynamically performs app security, and health monitors aligned with external systems.
Automation and Orchestration Capability	Vendor has application hosting location and access to its provisioning.	Vendor periodically modifies application configurations (including location and access) to meet relevant security and performance goals.	Vendor apps will inform device and network parts of changed state.	Vendor apps adapt dynamically to security and performance changes.
Governance Capability	Vendor legacy policies and manual enforcement for software dev and all other associated work.	Vendor begins to automate policy enforcement for application development (including access to development infrastructure), deployment, software asset management, ST&E at technology insertion, patching, and tracking software dependencies based on mission needs (e.g., with Software Bill of Materials).	Vendor's policies are current and have centralized enforcement mechanisms.	Vendor's policies are current and are dynamically and centrally updated and enforced.

Pillar 5: Data   Data ZT maturity is demonstrated as the vendor transitions from manual processes and static controls into automated processes with enforcement of policy automated and deep analysis.

Function	Traditional	Initial	Advanced	Optimal
Data Inventory Management	Vendor has manual process for tracking data that is lightly managed.	Vendor begins to automate data inventory processes for both on-premises and in-cloud environments, covering most vendor data, and begins to incorporate protections against data loss.	Vendor has some automatic process for data tracking, but still mainly manual.	Vendor has continual inventory, tagging, and tracking and leverages ML tools.
Data Categorization	Vendor employs limited and ad hoc data categorization capabilities.	Vendor begins to implement a data categorization strategy with defined labels and manual enforcement mechanisms.	Vendor automates some data categorization and labeling processes in a consistent, tiered, targeted manner with simple, structured formats and regular review.	Vendor automates data categorization and labeling enterprise-wide with robust techniques; granular, structured formats; and mechanisms to address all data types.
Data Availability	Vendor primarily makes data available from on-premises data stores with some off-site backups.	Vendor makes some data available from redundant, highly available data stores (e.g., cloud) and maintains off-site backups for on-premises data.	Vendor primarily makes data available from redundant, highly available data stores and ensures access to historical data.	Vendor uses dynamic methods to optimize data availability, including historical data, according to user and entity need.
Data Access	Vendor uses static controls to govern access to data.	Vendor begins to deploy automated data access controls that incorporate elements of least privilege across the enterprise.	Vendor provides least-privilege controls.	Vendor uses dynamic, just-in-time, least-privilege, and continuous risk-based decisions.

Function	Traditional	Initial	Advanced	Optimal
Data Encryption	Vendor's data is primarily on-prem and much data can be unencrypted.	Vendor encrypts all data in transit and, where feasible, data at rest (e.g., mission-critical data and data stored in external environments) and begins to formalize key management policies and secure encryption keys.	Vendor's data is in the cloud and encrypted at rest.	Vendor encrypts all data at all locations.
Visibility and Analytics Capability	Vendor has minimal data inventory with little visibility and analytics.	Vendor obtains visibility based on data inventory management, categorization, encryption, and access attempts.	Vendor's data is in inventory, batch updated, and analytics are basic.	Vendor is continually updating inventory, which provides robust analytics.
Automation and Orchestration Capability	Vendor has no consistent categories and labels, and hence no automation or orchestration.	Vendor uses some automated processes to implement data lifecycle and security policies.	Vendor schedules audits to locate high-value data with analysis; has limited orchestration and automation.	Vendor auto enforces access controls, ensures redundancy of all high-value data, and inventories auto updated.
Governance Capability	Vendor enforces data protection via admin controls, and most oversight is manual.	Vendor defines high-level data governance policies and relies primarily on manual, segmented implementation.	Vendor has some technical and admin controls, with data categories and access defined to integrate disperse data sources.	Vendor has full auto enforcement of data protection aligned with policy dynamically.

Cross-cutting Capabilities   Across all the pillars there exists a sub-layer of cross-cutting capabilities, Visibility and Analytics, Automation and Orchestration, and Governance, which should be integrated across each of the pillars. These cross-cutting capabilities can be visualized with Figure 3.1 from the CISA site.

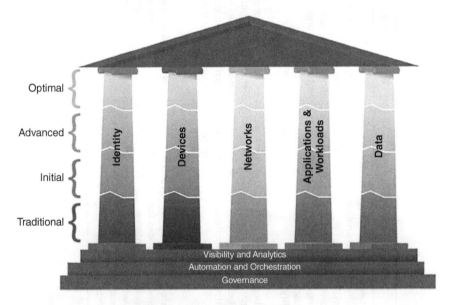

FIGURE 3.1 Zero Trust Maturity Model Pillars

Function	Traditional	Initial	Advanced	Optimal
Visibility and Analytics	Vendor manually collects limited logs across their enterprise with low fidelity and minimal analysis.	Vendor begins to automate the collection and analysis of logs and events for mission-critical functions and regularly assesses processes for gaps in visibility.	Vendor expands the automated collection of logs and events enterprise-wide (including virtual environments) for centralized analysis that correlates across multiple sources.	Vendor maintains comprehensive visibility enterprise-wide via centralized dynamic monitoring and advanced analysis of logs and events.
Automation and Orchestration	Vendor relies on static and manual processes to orchestrate operations and response activities with limited automation.	Vendor begins automating orchestration and response activities in support of critical mission functions.	Vendor automates orchestration and response activities enterprise-wide, leveraging contextual information from multiple sources to inform decisions.	Vendor orchestration and response activities dynamically respond to enterprise-wide changing requirements and environmental changes.
Governance	Vendor implements policies in an ad hoc manner across the enterprise, with policies enforced via manual processes or static technical mechanisms.	Vendor defines and begins implementing policies for enterprise-wide enforcement with minimal automation and manual updates.	Vendor implements tiered, tailored policies enterprise-wide and leverages automation where possible to support enforcement.	Vendor implements and fully automates enterprise-wide policies that enable tailored local controls with continuous enforcement and dynamic updates.

Zero Trust Maturity Assessment for Critical Vendors   From the preceding tables, you can glean a series of questions that you can ask your critical vendors to determine their ZT maturity level. Because this level of scrutiny can be exhausting for a vendor, reserve it for third parties that are critical for operations or the highest risk to your organization. After you have identified the vendors that your organization wants to include in the ZT journey, it is important to create a policy and process that clearly defines your organization's expectations regarding standards, policies, procedures, and assessments for these vendors.

Zero Trust Vendor Questionnaire

Using the tables provided on the CISA maturity assessment, you can design the questionnaire as either a remote assessment or a physical validation assessment. In a remote assessment, the questionnaire is sent to the vendor for them to fill out and send back for your team to evaluate. In a physical validation, your cybersecurity experts query the vendor directly and expect to see proof that the vendor has policies around the controls and can prove they run them in practice with physical evidence.

For organizations that are still maturing their overall third-party risk management (TPRM) program or just starting a ZT evaluation process for their vendors, a remote assessment is adequate. Design the questionnaire to be in clear business terms (no acronyms) to ensure little time back and forth with vendor on terminology or definitions. It should also have input validation or only allow for certain responses to ensure consistency in responses wherever possible. Because a ZT journey is not always easy to discern and vendors tend to overstate their security posture, understand that the veracity of the responses should be considered. Not to say they should be discounted, but between the fogginess of ZT steps and the fact that the vendor is self-answering, be ready to find gaps should you later on perform a physical validation.

More-mature organizations should aim to conduct physical validations for these assessments. Even less-mature organizations can benefit from initiating physical validation programs focused on a ZT approach. Because physical validation requires more resources and time compared to remote assessments, you should allocate this level of due diligence to only a select few vendors. An already existing physical validation questionnaire, based on any common cybersecurity framework (NIST-CSF, ISO 27001, etc.), would cover much of what is asked in the maturity assessment for ZT. The option would be to take that existing question set and focus only on the ZT pillars or leave it as is but ensure those specific questions are covered.

Whether your organization's physical validation approach involves a checklist or a conversation determines how the questions are addressed. Although a conversation-based method is preferred, if your organization relies on a checklist to ensure consistent questioning, you should exclude any non-ZT-related questions, unless they are required by regulatory or policy obligations. It is important to validate this based on your sector and regulatory oversight, although it is unlikely to happen considering the broad coverage of ZT principles. Question sets are often too long already, and when your team follows the questions around the five pillars as previously laid out, you'll likely end up with many of the same questions already there (with only the non-ZT items left out).

Physical validation is best accomplished using a conversation-based model. The theory here is that relying solely on a checklist, with your analyst's head buried in that checklist, with little to no eye contact or ability to follow a lead, does not prove very informative with regard to a security program's effectiveness.

It is a compliance exercise, which is not the same as cybersecurity. Engaging in a conversational format for asking questions during physical validations enables eye contact and fosters trust, even in virtual settings (where cameras should be encouraged to be turned on). This approach empowers experienced cyber third-party risk practitioners to effectively pursue leads as they arise. My first book, *Cybersecurity & Third-Party Risk: Third Party Threat Hunting* (Wiley, 2021), goes into detail about how to create this type of questionnaire. For now, though, let's take a few minutes to explore an example from the CISA maturity assessment and use the Data Pillar 5, Encryption row, as a template for formulating relevant questions.

Function	Traditional	Advanced	Optimal
Encryption	Vendor's data is primarily on-prem and many can be unencrypted.	Vendor's data is in the cloud and encrypted at rest.	Vendor encrypts all data at all locations.

Question Set

1. Does your organization have an encryption policy or standard?

   (a) If no, this means the vendor does not have a repeatable process and does encryption ad hoc. While rare, this is not unheard of based on experience.

   (b) If yes, what is the frequency of updates per the policy? And confirm it has been kept.

      i. Assessor views some proof in production/practice

   (c) Assessor should review document and ask questions based on the sections within the policy or standard.

      i. Assessor views some proof in production/practice

(d) Does the encryption algorithm standard meet industry standards?

    i. Assessor views some proof in production/practice

(e) Does it distinguish between on-prem and cloud/vendor standards?

    i. Assessor views some proof in production/practice

(f) How do they identify sensitive data to be encrypted and ensure that all that data is encrypted to standard? Is it automated or manual?

    i. Assessor views some proof in production/practice

More questions can be added to this section, but this should be sufficient to get most teams started. As the assessor moves down these questions, there should be a request to see some physical validation of the requirement or policy. After the physical validation has finished, the evaluation questionnaire, whether in a spreadsheet or a front end, should include an automated calculation of maturity based on the identified risk gaps or controls identified by the assessor.

How to Incentivize Vendors to Take Zero Trust Steps   Most TPR practitioners and vendors are experiencing "fatigue" with all the questionnaires and assessments. Approaching a vendor with another level of security oversight or requirements labeled "zero trust for our organization's vendors" could prove to be a challenging sell to both vendors and internal business partners. Here are some suggestions on how to approach this to reduce the necessary oversight and encourage vendors to adopt the ZT strategy.

Because this is for a small number of critical vendors, for the first iteration, narrow it to a vendor or two as a way to learn. As a way to incentivize vendors to adopt and so that business owners do not roll their eyes at yet another security request, lower the number and frequency of assessments required. For example, a vendor that participates in the ZT assessments and is successfully assessed at least at an Advanced stage of maturity only has to get assessed every other year, not annually. The argument in favor of this is because the vendor has been assessed to be at a level that your organization feels comfortable with on the ZT maturity scale, the blast radius is minimized and so the risk is reduced enough to not need an annual security assessment. If a vendor can get to the Optimal maturity level, that vendor may qualify for only annual attestations that there have been changes to their environment to lower that score (or only every five years they are reassessed). These all depend on your organization's risk appetite and your imagination as to how to not only promote the adoption of your requirements but also lower your own team's work when assessing vendors. When a vendor can get to the Advanced or Optimal stages of ZT maturity, it is reasonable to begin to make trade-offs in how often risk assessments are done, given their relative maturity.

Part I: Zero Trust and Third-Party Risk Explained Summary

The first part of this book sought to provide readers a common understanding of ZT, TPRM, and cyber third-party risk (CTPR) management to ensure everyone starts at same point. You then read deeper details about how to plan and implement a ZT strategy with a TPR. This would require the organization to determine TPR is their starting target (or next target) for a ZT journey. As you also learned, in collaboration with your internal networking, cyber operations, threat teams, and others, depending on your size and complexity, you can focus using the ZT and TPR OSI model by column and row on each segment. Another method of ZT in TPR discussed in this first part is to select a few key critical vendors and track their ZT strategy and journey. There is a simple set of questions that can be asked, or a more mature question set can be developed using the CISA Zero Trust Maturity assessment geared to vendors.

Part II of this book explores the implementation of the strategies and processes discussed in Part I through the example of KC Enterprises, a fictional company introduced in my first book. This is a mid-sized company, enabling readers to adapt the concepts to their own requirements, whether they need to scale up or down.

Apply the Lessons from Part I

KC Enterprises: Lessons Learned in ZT and CTPR

Part I of this book provides details on zero trust (ZT) and third-party risk (TPR), but it can be challenging to translate this information into practice and production in your organization. Part II of this book provides a guide as to how a company or organization can make the changes necessary to complete a ZT journey in TPR. This part discusses some techniques and tools, but the majority of the work centers on process and program changes to make ZT work for TPR. As mentioned before, ZT is not a technology or tool. Instead, it is a set of principles and goals, leveraging technology and tools, to achieve a reduced area of exposure when a breach occurs. The following examples are recommendations and ideas for how to translate and leverage what has been learned in the first part of the book into practice at your organization.

In my first book, *Cybersecurity and Third-Party Risk: Third Party Threat Hunting* (Wiley, 2021), I created a fictitious company to provide some hands-on examples of how to implement the process and practice. For this current book, some basic information about this fictional company is provided in the following sections.

Kristina Conglomerate Enterprises

Kristina Conglomerate (KC) Enterprises is a medium-size U.S.-based company with some offshore resources in the European Union, India, and the Philippines. It sells widgets all over the United States and requires its vendors to ship products and manage its inventory, factories, customer service, business processing, human resources, finance, and marketing, in addition to all typical corporate functions.

Based in Raleigh, North Carolina, KC has over 5,000 employees, mostly employed in the factories in North Carolina, and the corporate office downtown employs a couple hundred. Much of the non-factory staff are located in the corporate headquarters in Raleigh and in a large office in St. Louis that manages the factory in Missouri (which handles all widget distribution west of the Mississippi). Because KC makes the best widgets, there is a high demand on customer service and support, and therefore there are customer support centers outsourced to third parties in Ireland, the Philippines, and India to enable support for customers in any time zone around the world without interruption. In addition, KC has outsourced some business processing to India for financial processing.

KC has expanded in the last 10 years, mostly by acquiring other smaller widget manufacturers. However, some strategic purchases of the vendors who make some of the components for widgets have also occurred. Five years ago, KC made a large purchase of an up-and-coming software widget maker pre-IPO (that is, before a company goes public and is traded on a stock exchange). The widget maker is based in San Jose, California, and located in the heart of Silicon Valley, which is where much innovation for the company started. It can be a challenge for KC's cybersecurity team because it tends to view boundaries as more of a dare or a challenge.

For the past 20 years, KC has been expanding its footprint into digital widgets. These widgets do not involve any manufacturing processes but rely on IT assets like data centers to assist backend application developers in generating fresh demand for the digital widgets. KC also utilizes mobile applications to allow customers to directly purchase digital widgets on their smartphones and electronically send them to their friends and family. This has forced KC Enterprises to adopt several different changes and frameworks. Cybersecurity adopted the National Institute of Science and Technology Cybersecurity Framework (NIST-CSF) as the model, as is typical in many commercial environments. In addition, it matured its technology operations and management.

KC has a CIO and CISO; both report directly to the CEO of the firm. It is a public company, and its CEO reports to the board of directors. There is a technology risk committee on the board, and the CISO provides reports directly to them at regular intervals or earlier when circumstances require. Remote staff are scattered across the United States, with the support infrastructure growing massively in March 2020 due to the pandemic. The company will likely have fewer people in-office post-COVID, as some decisions to scale back on office (nonproduction) space is beneficial for the bottom line. (Note that the exact staffing levels and items are less important in this company than providing a consistent yardstick when doing the examples. Whether your firm is smaller and simpler or larger and more complex than KC Enterprises, the sizing and complexity of implementing the items in this book can be adjusted.)

KC has four types of data classification: public, internal, confidential, and restricted. KC policy dictates that all data internal and above (i.e., not public) must be encrypted. Internal data may be encrypted at the lower level of AES-128, but the top two must be at AES-256 or higher.

KC Enterprises manages its TPR and cybersecurity programs as separate teams. Third-party risk management (TPRM) reports to finance from the CFO, and the cybersecurity program reports to the CISO, who reports to the CEO. The CFO and CISO are peers. TPRM and cybersecurity have their own program and policy statements for their respective areas. Cybersecurity consists of several domains: identity and access management (IAM), architecture, cloud security, governance, risk and compliance, cyber ops, and reporting. As is typical, the cyber third-party risk (CTPR) team is located within governance, risk, and compliance (GRC), which is responsible for overseeing overall governance, enterprise risk management, and compliance with regulations. This placement is due to the perception that CTPR is primarily a compliance-related function. The company has several oversight committees and regulators that keep tabs on TPR and cybersecurity.

At KC Enterprises, the CTPR standards and policies are clear about what the two triggers are for when cybersecurity due diligence is required:

- The vendor will have, process, use, store, or transmit KC Enterprise customer or employee data that is of the top-three data classifications.

- The vendor will have a connection to any KC Enterprise network, whether intermittent or persistent.

As described, KC creates physical and digital widgets— pretend items designed to mimic a thriving business. The regulations for data protection have been adequately described as near universal, no matter what business or operation. The point isn't what KC makes or the services it provides. The risk isn't what your firm or company makes or creates; the risk is in the data you share with vendors or the connectivity you allow them. The use of this company example is to illustrate best practice to lower the risk third parties present to your firm.

KC Enterprises' Cyber Third-Party Risk Program

To run a successful CTPR program, documentation of governance, policy, procedures, and oversight must occur to ensure adherence to the program, although the KC Enterprises example we use also demonstrates the foundations of a program. The complexity or simplicity of the policy, processes, and other artifacts are dependent upon a host of differences at your organization.

KC Enterprises' Cybersecurity Policy

The cybersecurity policy document forms the basis for the scope of cybersecurity and the subprograms that it contains, such as cyber GRC, cyber operations, vulnerability management, and the other functions that run a modern technology-based company and economy.

Scope

Kristina Conglomerate Enterprises and its subsidiaries and affiliates (KC) cybersecurity policy (the "policy") is designed to accomplish the three pillars of confidentiality, integrity, and availability for all KC data and systems owned, operated, and managed by KC (the "assets"). The policy is intended to provide compliance with applicable regulations, laws, cybersecurity frameworks adopted, and higher-level KC policies and standards. A number of lower-level cybersecurity standards, procedures, and artifacts support and implement the policy.

The KC cybersecurity policy is designed to implement and support the cybersecurity program (the "program") as presented to the KC board of directors. The program implements and supports the policy's goals of the CIA triad to provide security to KC's information assets and systems. The supporting documentation of policies, procedures, and controls are the means to ensure the protection of those assets.

Breaches of the policy may result in disciplinary actions, up to and including termination of employment and legal action by KC if warranted.

Policy Statement and Objectives

The KC cybersecurity policy is designed to ensure the appropriate management review and approval of the program and to provide escalation avenues for cybersecurity risk from management to the board. It confirms the confidentiality, integrity, and availability of its data and assets; creates a baseline for audit, assessment, and regulatory compliance; and provides clear direction to employees, contractors, and any third party as to their due care and due diligence requirements around the assets.

Cybersecurity Program

The program provides confidentiality, integrity, and availability of all KC protected data (as defined in the "Classification of Information Assets" section that follows) from any disclosure, whether accidental or intentional. The program's implementation is risk based to align with risk appetite and risk priorities.

The program is based on the National Institute of Science and Technology Cybersecurity Framework (NIST-CSF) and is reassessed no less than annually to review its effectiveness and updates required due to environmental, financial, or business objectives. The program advances a defense-in-depth strategy to ensure a layered approach to the protection of the assets.

The program is periodically assessed by technology risk (second line), internal audit (third line), external auditors, regulatory supervisory agencies, and independent evaluations.

KC cybersecurity has the sole authority to create and modify physical, technical, and logical security standards and procedures to support the policy. While cybersecurity will consider business needs and objectives when enforcing these standards and procedures, it retains the sole authority to enforce them to ensure compliance with the policy. All lower-level standards, policies, procedures, and artifacts support the scope of the policy and carry the same authority as part of the program.

Classification of Information Assets

KC data classification provides a means for determining the risk of data. The following list describes the four classes of data and their relative risk to the organization:

- **Class 4 restricted**: This data is the most sensitive data at the company. Losing this data would be equivalent to losing the "crown jewels." It requires the highest level of available protection from misuse or loss. The access criteria must be set to a need-to-know basis and based on least privilege. The impact of loss or misuse would be serious and adverse to the company and cause severe reputational, financial, and/or strategic damages.

- **Class 3 sensitive:** These data assets are typically personally identifiable information (PII), operations, proprietary, and other information that if disclosed or misused would adversely affect the company, shareholders, customers, and partners with regulatory, financial, or reputational damage and penalties. The access criteria can be a bit broader than Class 4 but still should be on a need-to-know basis.

- **Class 2 internal:** These data assets are often internal and general business communications, documentation, and other items used in day-to-day business operations. The disclosure of this data would have very limited financial, reputational, or operational impact. Access is appropriate for all internal users at KC.

- **Class 1 public:** Data here is any data that can be found in public forums or online and does not require any protection. There must be no impact to KC or its shareholders if released. Access is open to all internal users and the public.

Now that you understand the basics for this company, let's use them as an example of how to implement ZT in TPRM.

A Really Bad Day

Maria C., the CISO for KC, was only in her third month in this role at the company when it happened. Of course, it happened on a Friday. It was late afternoon, around 4 p.m., when it wasn't quite the end of the business day but late enough on Friday that no one from the vendor would be around to answer questions until Monday. Notification of a security breach at a critical vendor was the subject line in the email, and then the text messages started from business leadership. JR Software, a vendor that performs key customer support functions, was hacked and had customer data and credit card information stolen. And it was ransomware, so the data wasn't available right now, which meant existing operations with them were suspended.

To add to the complexity, the email wasn't from the vendor, it came from the Incident Management team that noticed an online news article that mentioned JR Software as being "down" and internal sources reporting they are subject to a ransomware attack. Maria reached out to her CTPR leader, Lana, to inquire about a couple of items from her team. First, she needed to know if her manager was aware of the breach, if she had an analyst assigned to lead the effort, if there was a contact in the system of record for them to contact, and if someone could pull the existing contract to determine their obligations for incident notification.

Meanwhile, a conference call invite was sent out that included the CIO, CISO, the cyber incident management leaders, lead counsel, TPRM leadership, and the line-of-business leadership. The invite went out at 5:15 p.m. Friday afternoon, so some of the invitees were not online to see the calendar invitation. This resulted in a lot of frantic searching for mobile numbers and calls or text messages to get them on this call. As the team started to get on the call, there were a lot of nervous questions and not many answers. The line of business was unclear about the status of the contracts, and no one could get ahold of anyone from the vendor. Multiple calls to their normal contacts went unanswered, so there was no immediate knowledge of whether KC Enterprises data was impacted. However, the bigger issue is that the online portal run by JR Software was not running, and so calls were coming into corporate offices from angry customers because they were unable to order new or replacement products or parts.

As the call progressed, Maria got an update from Lana on the contracts and research on what the vendor had in terms of data and types. Unfortunately, it was discovered that the master service agreement (MSA) had not been updated for almost five years and they had no terms and conditions (T&Cs) for information security or privacy. Additionally, there was no language on incident management that required them to notify KC Enterprises in the event of a breach or incident. In terms of data, the vendor has the following data elements for all customers, up to five years history:

- Full name
- Month and day of birth (not year)
- Address
- Phone number(s)
- Products and parts purchased (five-year history)
- Credit card information

This information was given to the team on the call. The corporate counsel was livid that there were no incident management terms and wondered aloud about the idiot who allowed those terms to be agreed on. Maria reminded him that five years or more had passed since the MSA was last touched, so no one on this call was in their roles at that time. This would be a topic of the postmortem, Maria informed the audience on the phone, and told them to focus on current facts so that decisions could be made about next steps.

It was already almost past 6 p.m. on the call, and the team could gather no more information at this point. The decision was made for action items and owners, along with follow-up calls the next day. The supplier manager was assigned to continue to email, call, and in any way possible to get ahold of their contact at the vendor while the cyber team and others also attempted to get into contact with their known points of contact at the vendor.

This activity was to continue into the evening as late as reasonable and then pick up in the morning. The team agreed to meet again in the morning, and Maria placed her cyber threat team manager, Robert, in charge of the effort. Normally it would be an analyst (individual contributor), but given the size, complexity, potential impact, and large unknowns, a more seasoned person was needed to take the lead. Robert set up a meeting with the extended team, now called JR Tiger Team, for every morning at 8 a.m. for the next two weeks as a way to meet, discuss progress on any deliverables or questions, and coordinate communications and responses.

Then the Other Shoe Dropped

It started right after everyone dropped from the conference call: messages from the cyber threat team that there is anomalous behavior in one of the applications and databases, so they had to isolate it. The first text was ominous: "Boss bad behave in the payroll db, shutting down." After a few late-evening text messages back and forth to the manager, Robert, for the cyber threat team, called Maria directly to discuss the situation. The conversation was short but informative. The security information and event management (SIEM) team had reached out to Robert to indicate they were getting alarms on the location of the login for a user on the payroll database. Normally the user logs in from the United States, but this was coming from Eastern Europe, so they shut down the login but not before there was some data exfiltrated. The extent of the exfiltration was not known yet, but the team was investigating. Maria indicated for him to do his best to get updates as the team worked and to send them to her via email with any new developments. She also emailed the business owner and the database administrator for the payroll database to let them know of the incident, and she told Robert to include them in the ongoing meetings. The rest of her evening was spent documenting and creating lists for next steps of her own, then off to a fairly sleepless night.

The next day at 7 a.m., Maria's alarm went off, and although happy she got some sleep, it was clear from her phone next to her that a lot of activity was happening overnight. There were texts from Robert with updates as to knowledge about what happened to the payroll database. After a quick cup of coffee and a shower, it was time to log in to the daily JR Tiger Team meeting at 8 a.m. There were a good deal of updates from the team on the progress of the payroll database, but the supply management team and the human resources team could not get a return call from any of their normal contacts. In addition, there was human resource work that needed to be completed on Monday, and much not completed on Friday, which was a growing concern for management. The HR leader, a no-nonsense woman, got her team to assume the worst and begin to figure out how to work without the HR software short term.

The attention was then on the impact to the payroll database and determining whether the two incidents were somehow related. The CEO remarked that it did seem too coincidental, but not being a cyber expert, she deferred that to the team. At this point, there was no good idea of how it happened, but it appears an administrative user from JR Software, who has access to validate payroll with human resources online software, logged in shortly after 5 p.m. local time, but this user was from Eastern Europe, according to the geolocation teams. It was highly likely, according to the research, this was either the same team that broke into JR Software and stole the credentials, or they had already sold the credentials on to another individual or team, and they were already using it. Either way it appears that the JR Software breach is linked to the incident at KC Enterprises.

The specific type and quantity of data that was exfiltrated is still being determined. However, it is worth noting that the logs for the payroll database are not tuned to capture all potential data points. The team is looking at the size and tags for the previous day's versions of the payroll database to compare it with what is there now to determine what was copied or downloaded or both. The Saturday meeting ended with an agreement for the cyber and payroll teams to continue to work together on finding what was impacted, along with the supplier manager and human resources team working to get a response from the vendor.

Sunday's 8 a.m. meeting provided no more information and was very quick. When the workweek started, the expectation is that they would be able to get a response from JR Software, and the cyber team agreed to hire a specialized consultant to determine the extent of breach or event with the payroll database. It was also agreed to bring in another consulting firm to assist with the postmortem of why, who, what, and how much, as well as to offer suggestions about how to reduce the risk of a repeat event or events.

By Monday afternoon, the consultant teams were identified, and paperwork was making its way through the process for approvals and budget needs. The vendor was still refusing to answer any questions about the event, and the HR team was doing a mad scramble to find a manual way to process payroll and human resource activities while another team in HR was trying to find another vendor sometime in the near future. KC Enterprises' technical and management leadership were clear that they were not in the business of creating software for human resources, and a new vendor must be found for the long-term stability and growth of KC.

As the days and weeks went by, the data and readouts from the consultants were presented to the senior leadership first for an overview. With no contact from the vendor, the human resources team focused on getting the required items running and had located a large vendor that could take over very quickly with a cloud deployment (software-as-a-solution [SaaS]) that leveraged the data just prior to the event at JR Software. In addition, the consultant team that was evaluating the impact of the event on the payroll database determined that although the attacker had gained access at the privileged level, it appears that the access team cut them off before any copying or exfiltration could occur. This was good news, but the fact that the attacker gained access at all was still a high-value item needing to be solved.

Two weeks and a few days after the incident, JR Software issued a press release that gave more insight into the event. The CEO was interviewed by a business reporter, and he had clearly been coached by corporate counsel, given the tightness of some of his answers. Nonetheless, there was enough information to determine that JR had not enforced multifactor authentication (MFA) for its privileged users, and their password policy permitted 90 days before requiring a change. More importantly, it was revealed that for the administrator account that was breached, the user had reused the same password for as long as the investigative team could find. It was determined that JR Software password policy did not have a minimum password age. Even though the vendor password history policy was six passwords, this lack of a minimum password age allowed a user to cycle through all six passwords to arrive back at their "original" password (likely preferred and universally used by them).

A look into the payroll database revealed similar issues with the access controls. The consultants determined the access controls were not integrated into the Active Directory for the domain, meaning they were only local accounts, which allowed users to retain passwords with no changes required. There was a lot of activity around this discussion of the lack of integration into the domain policy for the access management, but it appears this was done so long ago that no one can remember who or why this was done.

The consulting companies were able to produce their reports on the root causes for both the JR Software and the KC payroll database. Much of the report was couched in polite language to soften the impact, but Maria got the point:

- KC Enterprises does not perform sufficient due diligence on their critical third parties.
- KC Enterprises does not have sufficient terms and conditions with critical vendors for incident response and management terms.
- KC Enterprises does not have proper processes to review vendor contracts on a regular basis to ensure compliance with best practice and regulatory guidance.
- KC Enterprises does not have adequate access management policies, processes, and controls for third parties.
- KC Enterprises does not have adequate controls to prevent lateral movement of an attacker.
- KC Enterprises does not have sufficient correlation of activities or processes for third-party vulnerabilities and risks within SIEM or other detective/preventive controls.

While the number of findings was only a handful, they entailed large gaps that the leadership team struggled to resolve. As the team discussed how to best solve for all the issues listed, it occurred to Maria, as the CISO, that many of the issues aligned with a ZT approach. She was already in the planning stages for a

ZT journey for KC Enterprises. The general concept had already been discussed with the CIO and CEO, along with the CFO to discuss budgeting needs. Originally the plan for ZT entailed focusing on internal "crown jewels" as a starting point and ZT focused on internal users. However, given the issues raised with the vendor controls, she started putting together a plan to have the focus shift to the TPR domain for first deployment of ZT.

5

Plan for a Plan

M aria's plan for the deployment of zero trust (ZT) into the third-party risk (TPR) domain would require a multidiscipline team across technology, networking, data loss prevention (DLP), third-party risk management (TPRM), architecture, and likely more. This was going to require a project manager to drive it, and she needed someone who could execute but also manage these different teams and leaders. Jimmy, the project manager chosen, was a long-time veteran of KC Enterprises and project management in general Jimmy would start by developing scope, schedule, budget, and resources plans to align with the strategic goals of the plan.

KC's ZT and CTPR Journey

Jimmy begins by nailing down the scope and schedule. The initial scope is defined as "Deploy zero trust principles and strategy to the third-party risk domain" with the schedule being done in phases. The phases are aligned to deployment plans: First is to define the protect surface, which is intended to help ensure the teams know what is in scope to get ZT, but more importantly, what is not in scope. Next is to map transaction flows to have the assurance that all traffic and activity by vendors is inventoried. Taking the protect surface and map transaction flows output, the architecture team will provide an architecture for how ZT is deployed. Once the architecture is developed and approved, the team will begin to deploy ZT policies. These policies are not just technical policies but also updates to standards, policies, and procedures. The last step is to design a monitor and maintain a process that not only captures what the current state of ZT and TPR but also allows for continuous improvement with this information.

Like most projects Jimmy had done before, he was given some preferred end dates that the CISO and leadership would like to see for implementation. The timeline given was to be in the monitor and maintain stage by the end of one year from project start. It was already the end of December at the time of the initial planning, so Jimmy set the target date of the middle of March. This additional quarter would allow for the time he anticipated it would take for scope, schedule, budget, and resources to be approved, teammates assigned, and the project to perform formal kickoff.

Jimmy held the first meeting for the project, which was now called Project Expeditus (after Saint Expeditus, who is the patron saint of urgent causes). The initial team at the kickoff was attended by the CISO, CIO, network security leader, DLP leader, cloud security leader, governance, risk, and compliance (GRC) leader, legal leadership, cyber vulnerability management, and cyber operations leadership. Jimmy began by thanking everyone for attending and provided an overview of Project Expeditus. As a project manager, he designed a steering committee to guide the project's big decisions and deal with the big four categories (scope, resources, schedule, and budget):

- **Steering committee:** A project steering committee was established with the CISO, CIO, IAM (identity and access management) leader, DLP leader, network security leader, and the cyber operations leader. The steering committee is responsible for the success of the project as well as to maintain control of the scope, resources, schedule, and budget. The project sponsors are the CISO and CIO.

- **Scope:** The scope of Project Expeditus is confined to implementing ZT principles, process, and technology on third-party and fourth-party users, infrastructure, and workloads. What is not in scope is also important: Although there may be opportunities to apply ZT principles, process, and technology within our organization as they implement Project Expeditus, these are considered out of scope and will not be added unless approved by the steering committee for Project Expeditus.

- **Resources:** Due to the anticipated work required by teammates at KC Enterprises to be successful on the project, the steering committee approved the managers for any individual contributor involved in the project more than 50 percent of their time will be provided an offshore contractor (reporting to the manager) to ensure existing work does not stop or get overly delayed. It is anticipated that resources will be allocated by the managers as subject matter experts are identified. Given the priority of the project, any resource assigned more than 50 percent of their time will have their deliverables added to their annual performance goals and review. Specific resources will be identified as the project progresses.

- **Schedule:** The timeline for the project is one year from today. The schedule is broken into phases, and the methodology used will be waterfall. While it could be done with an agile methodology, there were not sufficient resources in place to manage an agile method, and most of the team is better accustomed to the waterfall methodology. It was decided it would be better to not add the training on agile methods on top of the work to implement ZT; it might be just too much for the teammates and send them "over the edge" with too much change.

- **Budget:** The funds for the project are not unlimited, but the CFO, who watched the financial fallout from the JR Software breach and its impact on KC Enterprises' bottom line for fourth quarter, is more than willing to fund the project. Initial estimates for amounts needed are not significant given many of the tools that already exist in the enterprise systems. In addition, much of the changes will be process and policy changes, which do not cost money, but time and training. The CFO put aside money for the resource backfills (contractors who will help out full time resources assigned more than 50 percent to Project Expeditus) and any anticipated additional licenses needed for the technologies used to enforce ZT principles.

Jimmy set up regular meetings for the steering committee and the core team for the project. The core team is primarily the team at the initial kickoff, but absent the steering committee members. The steering committee meets monthly, while the core team meets weekly. Other meetings will be scheduled as needed or required. A project website was created on the corporate collaboration site (on the KC Enterprises intranet) for sharing of all relevant documentation and information.

Zero Trust and Project Management

Project Expeditus is the name of the project for zero trust for third-party risk at KC Enterprises. Project planning and management are crucial to the success of any ZT deployment. This is for several reasons. First, ZT takes a while and a lot of effort. Second, ZT takes a village, to quote a former first lady. Success requires a multitude of disciplines across a multitude of teams, depending on the size and complexity of your program. KC did itself a favor getting a "seasoned" project manager in Jimmy, with the backing of a steering committee of senior leadership to ensure the backing at the appropriate level to make it a priority for their direct reports.

Define the Protect Surface

Defining the protect surface is an important first step in any ZT journey. In this case, because the project is focused on third-party domain, the scope of the protect surface is anything vendor or *nth*-party related. The protect surface in this case was defined as the critical data, assets, applications, and services. These are controlled by the three main areas listed: third-party users, third-party applications, and third-party infrastructure. As the team began to do research on what is included in this list of areas of focus, the team engaged with each of the domain owners on how best to understand the surface to define and protect.

The effort to determine what the protect surface is required several meetings that Jimmy held to get this information out of the team. The starting point was to explain that the protect surface needs to be finite and small. Initial meetings, as expected, began with some wide discussions of what that definition is, and it was a bit of a rathole and not productive. Jimmy struggled with how to steer the team back to making the protect surface fit the guidelines. It was decided that any items added to the protect surface must be reviewed and approved by the steering committee. This step was explained to the core team for the project as well as anyone helping define what is in the protected area. That focused the participants a bit narrower as they realized their managers and leaders would be reviewing. Additionally, this step allows teammates to add items to the list of protected items, and if management disagrees, then they can make that decision at the appropriate level to not add.

The critical data, assets, applications, and services at KC Enterprises are currently not centralized or together, so the protect surface is distributed. A protect surface is not the entire attack surface of the organization; it is only those items that are viewed as most critical. In the case of KC Enterprises, this refers to any location where Class 3 and/or Class 4 data is stored, applications that are systemically critical for operations, and services required to run operations. The mapping of this data, applications, assets, and services produced the following listing:

- **Data**
  - **Customer databases:** There were five separate databases identified at KC Enterprises that contain sensitive (Class 3 and 4) data. Currently these are spread out in several business units and are not centrally managed for access or logging and monitoring.
  - **Intellectual property databases:** There are two databases internally that contain the plans and details about the widgets and e-widgets that KC Enterprises produces for customers. This data is their "secret sauce" and if

compromised could cause the company to lose its competitive advantage. This would lead to a potential collapse in sales and revenue.

- **Business and operations secrets:** This includes a number of databases and data blobs that store merger and acquisitions data, network maps, encryption keys, pricing lists, and employee personal information.
- **Cloud:** Two databases and a front end exist in the team's cloud deployment (to a cloud service provider). The data in this is customer data, and it is presenting data sitting behind in the KC Enterprises data center.

- **Applications**
  - **Customer front end:** This is the website where customers would log in to order, check on order status, pay for products or services, and file any customer issues with products. It currently sits in Amazon Web Services, while the data is hosted inside the company's data center.
  - **Human resources data:** This involves both the HR system (which is no longer the JR Software product) and the payroll database. Both of these systems are internal to KC's network but are not in the same network or physical location.
  - **Security information and event management (SIEM):** This tool is essential to the operation of ZT, and so it becomes critical.
  - **Data loss prevention:** This application is critical to the operations and success of ZT.
  - **KC product sizer:** This is an application that internal sales and marketing teams use to help larger customers size the number of widgets and/or e-widgets.

- **Assets**
  - These are the specific servers, network devices, and other assets used to manage and protect the data, applications, and services in the protect surface.
  - These are edge devices used to communicate with customers. This includes the hardware for network connectivity and telecommunications equipment.
- **Services**
  - **Critical network functions:** These include a number of items: mail servers, print servers, Domain Naming Service (DNS) servers, Dynamic Host Configuration Protocol (DHCP) servers, Active Directory (AD) servers, DLP systems, intrusion prevention systems, and the SIEM system.

This list of protect surface items is not focused on the entire attack surface for KC Enterprises. That is a goal that captures just those assets that need to be protected to operate and reduce the ability of an attacker to do more damage. This initial list that Jimmy collected was logged as the scope for Project Expeditus formally by the steering committee and on the collaboration intranet site.

Map Transaction Flows

Mapping the flow of transactions with these protect items was the next step in the project. This step is designed to find the transactions between users, applications, and data. The primary focus is on which applications have access to sensitive data, the users that have the access to this data and applications, and the users and applications that have access to infrastructure.

This step can be accomplished a number of ways, and the CISO allowed the project team to be creative to ensure they captured as much data as possible. First they leveraged existing architectural and flow diagrams already created to capture what is moving and where. For the customer and intellectual property databases, there were both high level and low level flow diagrams done as part of the architectural approval process for these to be deployed. Business and operations secrets did not have anything already, so the team had to develop a flow diagram for these. Some of them were not in central locations, so this proved difficult but not impossible. Their AWS deployment with the customer front end was already mapped out for transaction flows as part of the architectural review per process at KC Enterprises. However, because the team noticed the design of the flow didn't match how it was in production, changes were made to match existing flows.

Next the team placed a next-generation firewall (NGFW) into the network in "virtual wire" mode (also known as vwire), which provided views into flows. This technique allows a more passive but complete picture of flows into their traffic and where it is going. These NGFWs also enable traffic decryption while in transit, providing the team with visibility into the actual content of the traffic that they wouldn't have obtained otherwise. The network security team allowed this to run for a month to ensure as much intermittent traffic was captured as possible, and then they leveraged good-old spreadsheet technology to review and provide clarity on all the transaction flows. Given the amount of data, this proved too challenging for the team, so a data lake was developed with an already deployed artificial intelligence (AI) tool to map out the transactions more cleanly.

For the users, the team mapped out groups and users to the applications and data they need access to. They wanted to better understand the specific type and duration of access required for their work. Sometimes administrators need just read-only access, not read-write access. The goal was always to ensure least-privilege access, aligned with their business purpose. Application flows were mapped with both the application data and how the data is stored, encrypted, backed up, and destroyed when use is completed. Data workflows were designed to capture the flow of the data, but also who uses it and where the data is collected, stored, used, and transferred. In addition, data flows focused on how the data is encrypted, archived, and destroyed after use. Services mappings were aimed at how they flow across the environment. Lastly, infrastructure flow mapping was finding location, who uses the infrastructure, what it was used for, and how it fits into the workflows.

The transaction flows mapped out allowed the team to understand how to segment the network and where additional controls were required to implement ZT. In addition, as the team reviewed the mappings, it was clear that a number of inefficiencies had built up organically over the life of the network and deployments. This gave the team an opportunity to optimize these flows as well as make them more secure.

Architecture Environment

The Project Expeditus team, having determined what the protect surface is at KC Enterprises and then mapped out all the relevant transaction flows, was now able to begin the architecture steps to deploy ZT into their TPR space. This architecture work would involve moving assets, some moving physically and others moving logically. It would also require segmentation within the network, which was largely considered a "flat" network (meaning very little segmentation). The user access policies would have to be changed as well, but the first step was to determine how to best get to a microsegmentation end goal and protect the attack surface. See Figure 5.1.

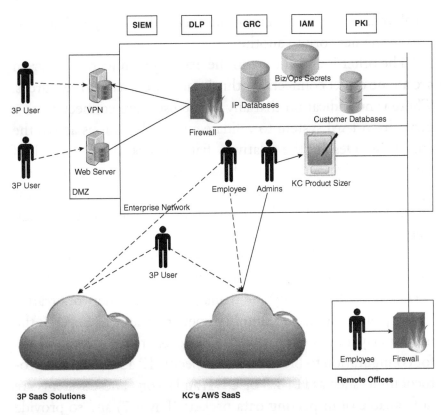

FIGURE 5.1 KC's Enterprises' architecture pre-zero trust

The existing architecture had several gaps that were going to make the move to ZT problematic and challenging. First, all the elements critical to the management and orchestration are above the enterprise; these are the SIEM, DLP, GRC, IAM, and PKI (public key infrastructure) elements. While they are running in the network, they are not operating over a large enough area and are not coordinated well enough to detect issues broadly. There is not a protected area, called a *trusted zone*, where all the important secrets are kept and isolated. Notice all the databases containing valuable information, such as customer data and intellectual property, are connected to the main network plane, along with connections to remote offices. No segmentation to speak of and only a minimum number of hops to get from one area of the network to another.

The other items of note in the existing architecture diagram are all the direct connections third-party users have to resources. There is no indication that any of the users are connecting to a centralized IAM system to validate and track sessions across the enterprise. Despite the relatively flat network, there is a lack of synchronization across it for how users access and from where they are accessing it. It shows vendor users, even administrator level, connecting directly to resources without going through some central IAM process.

There is very little sophistication in the network, including the use of "firewalls" rather than NGFWs that provide a much needed boost to visibility and management of all network traffic. These plain firewalls are simply inspecting traffic at Layer 3, the network layer of the OSI model. This level of firewall only allows for configuration to block or allow specific IP addresses and protocol limits such as HTTP or UDP, and so on. These systems are not capable of inspecting data packets (Layer 7) and so provide no visibility into the context or risk of the traffic itself. These firewalls can also provide granularity on ports, but again this is not specific enough for a ZT deployment of capabilities. The architecture team realized they had a lot of redesign to complete to enable a ZT journey. The actual work would need to be done in stages and involve a number of operations and technology teams. Hardware would need to be moved around, some removed and retired, and all new equipment ordered. This new equipment and software meant a review by the architecture review board (ARB) and also training on these new systems by the existing engineers.

The first step was to have a design principle in the architecture, and that was to have segmentation gateways around the areas requiring protection. As they looked at how the data, applications, assets, and services were deployed in the current enterprise, the decision was to move many of these objects behind segmentation gateways that were unique to their use cases. This would allow for very specific rules and alerts based on these use cases and, given this specificity, was less likely to throw false-positive alarms in the future. For example, the customer database needed to be available at all hours and globally, because KC Enterprises customers were global and the team didn't want to restrict when a customer could buy a widget. In contrast, the intellectual property database should be available only from inside the network (the customer database was available externally via their AWS connector) and normally during business hours in the United States. These two databases would be placed behind separate segmentation gateways to ensure scalability, minimize the risk of a single point of failure, and apply customized rulesets based on their specific use cases.

The segmentation gateways will enforce policies, decrypt traffic as necessary, inspect all traffic, and apply any security services for outbound communications, including blocking any malicious traffic trying to enter the protect surface area. The decrypted traffic will be inspected as it transits the gateway for better visibility into what is traversing it, but they will also be logging all traffic from Layer 2 to Layer 7. These logs will be forwarded to the SIEM tool for near-real-time analysis. The segmentations are next generation and allowed for user and group-based policy enforcement by connecting them to the LDAP on the Active Directory servers. They had the option of using XML API to the directory server but declined that option as their second choice in terms of preference. This policy enforcement allowed the team to have policy rules that flowed from access control systems to these gateways. This must be managed with an eye toward scalability and latency as the ZT deployment progresses. Understanding that this planning may not be able to consider all types and volumes of traffic, the team will need to have a plan to "manage" this traffic flow to be optimal for business operations and security requirements.

The next architectural changes required placing all the security capabilities into a central control point to allow for aggregation of the policies. DLP tools and technologies, DNS protections, intrusion detection and prevention systems (IDS/IPS), secure web gateways (SWGs), cloud access security broker (CASB), vulnerability protection software and systems, and the SIEM were all assets and security capabilities that needed to be better positioned to take advantage of the changes. Figure 5.2 shows the results.

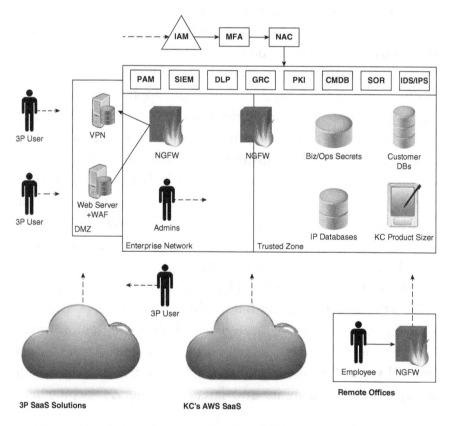

FIGURE 5.2 KC Enterprises' zero trust and third-party risk architecture

The difference between pre- and post-ZT changes is significant. As this is a high-level architecture, it outlines the approach and principles for the team's ZT journey. The largest change was to sever the environment into two spaces: enterprise network and trust zone, with the only access between the two being with an NGFW. The items that KC Enterprises had identified as their highest-risk items were all placed in the trusted zone: customer databases, business and operations secrets, intellectual property, and the KC product sizer. The logical controls placed to enter and stay in this zone were much higher than enterprise or any other place in the network. Creating a trusted zone also allows for the team to place additional items into this space as new high-risk, high-priority items are identified in any subsequent efforts.

All the required tools and processes that were outside or siloed in the previous architecture are now brought inside and across the enterprise. Privileged access management (PAM), security information and event monitoring (SIEM), data loss prevention (DLP), governance, risk, and compliance (GRC), public key infrastructure (PKI), configuration management database (CMDB), systems of record (SoRs), and intrusion detection and prevention systems (IDS/IPS) were all brought inside the network and now configured to speak to each other to provide the context needs for ZT. Many of these systems were not deployed at all, were in planning stages, or had minimal capabilities running across a minimal number of systems. Most were not integrated to talk to each other or provide data and logging material to any other system.

The PAM systems prior to the JR Software were confined to only KC teammates and contractors who worked directly for the organization. And the team had not purchased a commercial product to manage the privileged access at KC, but was leveraging a password vaulting product not really designed to use this way. However, management had not been convinced prior to the security incident of the importance of the risk for administrator access being managed so loosely. Upon examination in the post-mortem, it was discovered this system's highly manual process meant there were misses for compliance along the way. Many of these were found in the months before the JR incident, but the process of escalation had not worked correctly to highlight this gap. While the architecture was being worked out, the IAM team began the process to assess what their requirements were for this product and determine which commercial PAM product to purchase and implement. The PAM deployment will drive all privileged and elevated third-party access to the network through that process and tool. PAM will also be used as a bridge between network segments leveraging the NGFW.

The Network Access Control (NAC) was not deployed globally at KC Enterprises prior as well but was confined to areas where it was expected guests would be able to connect to wired or wireless networks. This was primarily in lobbies (main offices or remote) and a guest wireless system to ensure anyone connecting to the guest Wi-Fi did not introduce any malware. Deploying NAC to have device and user security postures checked prior to connecting, regardless of location, was key to ZT success. While the whole policy decision point process is not completed when IAM to multifactor authentication (MFA) to NAC has completed, this is considered the "gateway" to the rest of the systems below to provide the complete orchestration.

SIEM and DLP tools were deployed previously, but they were very siloed and not across the entire enterprise. These tools needed to be increased in terms of capabilities and sizing to allow for the huge increase in workload they would take in the new architecture.

Although the team considered deploying a software-defined perimeter (SDP), ultimately they decided to leverage that technology and solution in a future phase of ZT at KC Enterprises. The SDP solution would require architectural changes to some of KC's own internal applications, which required additional time to address. It is not unusual during a ZT journey to encounter delays in implementing an optimal solution, and decisions may be made to proceed without waiting for the absolute best solution.

The demilitarized zone (DMZ) persists in the new architecture, but the web server has gotten a much-needed web application firewall (WAF). A WAF will protect the web applications by filtering, monitoring, and blocking any malicious web traffic. These tools can also be configured to not allow any unauthorized data from leaving the web application. The WAF can be tuned and set with policies that determine what traffic is potentially malicious and what traffic is safe to allow. WAFs can come as software, an appliance, or even as a service in the cloud deployments. The example of placing the WAF here is obvious because it is in the DMZ, but the practice of deploying them (WAFs) to all other web services inside and outside the bank became policy and practice. The WAFs were all able to be updated via automatic updates from vulnerability management and the web operations teams at KC Enterprises.

One of the more obvious changes from the previous architecture is the lack of any direct connection to a resource by anything anymore. This is a reference to the fact that all access management activities would now be centralized into the operational "triangle" shape in Figure 5.2 at the top labeled IAM. In the parlance of a ZT deployment, this is typically referred to as the *policy decision point* (PDP). This term refers to the comprehensive concept of the combination of tools, processes, and teams that are integrated to provide the context-driven identity management system required in ZT. Note that the arrow going into the IAM triangle is dotted, and then all other resources (clouds, people, machines, and so on) have a similar dotted line coming from them. This in reference to the number of ways these resources can connect to the PDP system: Lightweight Directory Access Protocol (LDAP) and RADIUS for direct connections or Security Assertion Markup Language (SAML) or OAuth for indirect connections. Rather than prescribe which process to use for each, the architecture team developed patterns for each type of access to the PDP and IAM entry points. There are two key points to ensure the PDP can perform: that it can trust the data it receives from the identify provider via API or a public certificate so it can validate the data it receives; and that it can map attributes from the identity providers to allow it to pass the context-based requirements for ZT to work successfully.

As the IAM process is completed, there is a step to require MFA for all third-party users and resources connecting. As part of the written policy updates in the standards for IAM and third-party baseline standards, requirements were added that all vendors must have MFA for any access, whether it is an administrator or privileged account or what is considered a normal user account. The architecture team did not recommend a specific way to tackle the MFA requirement, which would allow for business and technology to find solutions that work best for their use cases. An architecture pattern would be developed to allow for them to offer preferred methods and reusable examples for business.

Remote office connections change as they no longer connect directly into the network backbone, and given the connection is not direct, it is not context based for the type of remote office. Previously, any remote office connected the same to the KC networks, and traffic was allowed two ways with little management or knowledge of what the traffic was doing. Now the team has placed an NGFW at every remote office to allow for Layer 7 inspection of traffic and has connected these more intelligent firewalls to the context system inherent in the PDP. This will allow for a remote office to vary from a home office, a warehouse, or a KC Enterprises widget service center. All three types of remote offices perform different things for the firm and therefore require access and permission unique for each. This meant the need to be context aware in how access is approached for each type of remote offices. Creating context-aware tools and systems to detect and manage this level was a required goal for the ZT deployment. The team asked why this was required given there aren't typically third-parties at the remote offices, except for physical visits. The reason given was this: Offshore resources and call centers would be placed into the "remote office" category going forward, and this allowed for handling this particular context use case.

The CMDB needed to be integrated into the overall enterprise architecture. Previously, there was no required inclusion of third-party products, workloads, or resources into the enterprise inventory. Given that many of these items were not inventoried, it was a risk that was not being monitored. As new devices are connected to the network, third party or directly owned by KC, they must be entered into the CMDB, and this talks directly to the NAC system via secure API to monitor and manage these resources. All third-party products were tagged in the system with TP in their metadata to help with categorization.

System of record (SoR) is a comprehensive term that refers to the information storage system serving as the authoritative source for a specific data element or information. In the third-party domain, which the initial ZT is focused on, this is the data management system that contains all vendor data, called a vendor management system (VMS). KC Enterprises uses a large commercial VMS that they have customized over time to meet their needs. Bringing the SoR into the whole PDP process allows the technology and steps to verify the validity of the vendor's active relationship. Second, the other SoR for vendors is the legal documentation system. This system contains all active and inactive master service agreements (MSAs) and all terms and conditions (T&Cs) for each vendor at KC Enterprises. These two systems talk to each other in a nightly batch job to ensure all active vendors in the VMS have active and up-to-date contract data. This was an upgrade to the system since the JR Software breach that was solved programmatically with the secure API connections to the two databases. Nightly, this batch runs, and if the tagging on the MSAs and T&Cs does not meet the date range given (the system checks that the age is not greater than three years), the system notifies appropriate stakeholders (supply manager, legal, business leadership) and requires a new contract to be started before any new or renewed business can be generated by the vendor.

The last piece of the architecture that required success for end-to-end integration was the ability of all the components to integrate via commonly used APIs and the ability to pass "tags" between them. These tags would be keys to identifying and providing the context throughout the system to allow both systems and process to make informed decisions. For example, there must be a way to pass a tag of 3P for anything that is identified as *third party* at KC Enterprises. Data traffic that traverses the network should be tagged as 3P for metadata as it moves or gets stored. A vendor-supplied and managed network appliance is tagged with 3P in the equipment inventory (CMDB), and that database is linked to the VMS database to validate the vendor has up-to-date contracts and T&Cs.

The architecture team took this all to the ARB for review and approval. The ARB is comprised of five voting members: chief technology officer, chief information officer, chief information security officer, principal engineer for security architecture, and principal engineer for enterprise architecture. The ARB usually meets once a month, and given the scope, complexity, and impact of the ZT effort, it was decided the team would present at the ARB initially and then provide a progress update monthly to the ARB. It was assumed that the architecture would need to be altered as deployments showed any weakness or trouble in production. Coming back with a regular meeting would allow for any changes or corrections to be discussed and captured as quickly as possible.

Once the ARB had reviewed and approved the architecture for ZT deployment, the handoff was done to the project team, and the individual owners for each domain were identified. The process of implementing these architectural changes was integrated into the project plan, with assigned owners and specific milestones.

Deploy Zero Trust Policies

Now that the team has developed a ZT architecture, they can take those plans and designs and use them to deploy the actual policies in production. This will be done in steps to allow for any issue resolution. There are no big-bang deployments in ZT usually, but instead measured deployment plans to allow for changes to be well designed and deployed. Many of the changes require user behavior changes, and this requires the ZT team to explain to that user community why the changes are occurring. The team started by planning how to make both logical and environmental changes.

Logical Policies and Environmental Changes

The changes to the environment to achieve ZT for TPR were done in steps to allow for the ability to troubleshoot issues as the deployment progressed. An all-at-once approach could lead to confusion about the root cause should anything go wrong during deployment. The CISO had introduced the OSI Zero Trust/Third Party Risk Model (see Table 5.1) early in the process to the project manager, Jimmy, and the team. The OSI model was used to help identify relevant constituent components from the resources and principles of ZT, which then aided in their development and implementation of ZT policies at KC Enterprises.

TABLE 5.1 Zero Trust and Third-Party Risk OSI Table

	Identity	Device/Workload	Access	Transaction
ZT for TP Users	Validate TP users with strong auth.	Verify TP user device integrity.	Enforce least-privilege access for TP users to data and apps.	Scan all content for TP malicious activity and data theft.
ZT for TP Apps	Validate TP developers, DevOps, and admins with strong auth.	Verify TP workload integrity.	Enforce least-privilege access for TP workloads accessing other workloads.	Scan all content for TP malicious activity and data theft.
ZT for TP Infra	Validate TP users with access to infrastructure.	Identify all TP devices (including IoT).	Enforce least-privilege access segmentation for third-party infra.	Scan all content within the infra for TP malicious activity and data theft.

*ZT = Zero Trust; TP = Third Party

Zero Trust for Third-Party Users at KC Enterprises

The architecture for ZT at the enterprise was clear about how IAM process was critical to the success of deployment and production use. A number of third-party users had access to critical systems at KC Enterprises, and with the protect surface identified and now all those items in the trusted zone (along with a better context of the end-to-end enterprise), it was possible to implement the changes to the who, what, when, where, and how of third-party user access.

Third-Party User and Device Integrity An inventory was done on the Active Directory accounts, and then the team had to start to break them out into human versus system accounts. Service or system accounts were those that were used by applications or hardware to operate and talk to the operating system and any required external hardware. These were being dealt with in the row below on the OSI model and are often handled this way in remediation or management teams in IAM. By sifting out the human accounts, they further sorted by teammates (full-time employees), contractors (directly employed by resource vendor), and third-party users. This was accomplished by taking the human resource database and comparing it with the contractors list. The leftover was validated a second time as the list of vendors with user accounts at KC Enterprises.

Using a federated access model, some of these accounts were not direct user accounts in the Active Directory but were from trusted sources. The new architecture and policy requirements meant all these trusted sources had to be validated and verified on a regular basis (varied based on the source type). These sources also now had to pass along all the required context information, such as vendor_name, source_address, unique_id, and others required based on how much access is required. For example, if the vendor and line of business know they will never require access to any protected assets, they may provide only minimal context information to save on time and resources. Others that will need access to the customer databases, in the trusted zone, must have the complete list of tags for context to gain access authorization or it will be denied automatically.

The list of vendors with a direct user account was reconsidered. The preferred model was the federated model so that it was a clear delineation between first party and third party. It was decided that this would be the standard pattern for the vendor user connectivity (again, service accounts may be handled differently), and the project undertook a subproject to migrate all those vendors with user accounts into the federated model with existing trusted sources (supplied to the vendors). When that wasn't possible, they were required to use a virtual desktop infrastructure (VDI) to connect to the network. This would isolate those few who couldn't use a federated model, who were then easily tracked in an environment where KC controlled the security and data protections. The project team had to be reminded that ZT is a journey that will sometimes require a long tail for some steps to completely close a task or goal.

As the network security team deployed NAC across the enterprise as part of the ZT project, the ability to better control access by user and device security posture became possible. As users were identified as third party, the NAC required certain attributes to ensure context was known about the vendor user (geolocation, vendor name, source, etc.) that was required for the access requested. NAC was now employed as part of the process for all connectivity to the KC network. If the vendor only wanted access to the guest Wi-Fi to connect to their own company's VPN, that was all provided and NAC checked what was required for that network. If the vendor required more direct access to a part of the network, the NAC was tuned to ensure that all appropriate tags were as expected (or access was denied) and that the security posture of the device or user meets requirements. NAC was deployed in stages to allow for "tuning" during the rollout. As it was successfully managed, they were able to provide a quarantine space for recognized third-party users or devices that did not meet a criteria. This allowed the appropriate team to take corrective action when necessary.

Third-Party Least-Privileged Access   As the identity and access is key to ZT success, it was a key step to change and improve the access control policies and procedures to better meet this goal. The tagging of vendor users allowed for their access controls to be altered to meet these goals without affecting other users (for now, as ZT was certainly going to target the overall enterprise next). The access controls for third-party user changes started with requirements on authentication methods. First, all third-party users were required to have MFA. Because all vendors should be in a federated model for initial authentication, the MFA is required to happen upon "handoff" from the trusted federated source to KC's authentication systems. MFA was offered primarily with the existing multifactor methods deployed at KC, which was an RSA token (hard or soft tokens were offered) or the Azure authenticator tool, but other methods were allowed via SAML or OAuth methods, with architecture and design patterns offered to vendors as required.

Next was an increase in the complexity requirements for third-party users. Vendors were required to have passwords of at least 12 characters, renewed every 60 days, minimum 1 day age, and 10 passwords in history. The password system was also upgraded to check for not only common dictionary words but also known compromised credentials, unacceptable words, or too-easy-to-guess passwords. These requirements were beyond what was expected of internal KC users, but it is typical to have external (third-party) higher standards or requirements than internal for the simple reason that they are not directly controlled by the enterprise.

In addition to tagging, the access controls included information that helped determine the when and where of access by third-party users. When a vendor connected to any resource within the network, it was essential to have the ability to control the when and where of their access. For example, the guest network had a fairly low bar for connectivity even with the NAC, but it did have a time control that denied access after late business hours. To allow for occasional late work by a vendor, it allowed for guest Wi-Fi access until 9 p.m. and then not before 6 a.m. Anything between 9 p.m. and 6 a.m. required a special-access request because it would be considered not business as usual to have anyone on the guest network past those times. However, the third-party user who is performing maintenance on the customer database is known to be offshore, and so the time constraint is actually the reverse to U.S. business operating hours.

Lastly, the logging and tracking of all third-party users was enhanced and further shared across the ecosystem for the PDP process. Previously, the logging was done minimally, if at all, for any users, but in particular on third-party users. Logging was enabled for nearly all activities involved in the IAM policy and process to allow for context but also more importantly so that any system doing monitoring and scanning could promptly access and use the logs. The logs are sent to a safe location in the trusted zone for review by many different operations (mainly the SIEM and DLP teams).

Third-Party User and Device Scanning   As the underlay for all three rows of types of third-party resources listed is the requirement to scan continually and with context. In this instance, the requirement is to ensure all third-party user interactions are being monitored and scanned for malicious activity. This is driven largely by the context of each user and the access level or resource the user is utilizing. As the third-party access risk escalates with their level of access, the logging is increased as well as the priority it receives in any monitoring process. Guest network access logs are only reviewed when, for example, a third party connects with malware and is sent to quarantine or denied access altogether. However, for access to more sensitive areas, a lot more triggers with lower thresholds would trigger a human intervention in many of the tools and process for monitoring. A vendor user might connect to the customer database at the end of his day in India, which is coming up on the 6 a.m. cutoff for access to the database. When 6 a.m. rolls around, it could cut off the access, but this is suboptimal, given the rule is not meant to be a hammer to prevent work from taking place. In this case, the system would start a workflow to notify the user that they are coming up on the limit to access (in this case due to business hour restrictions) and allow the user to notify an administrator to review and approve their access for a set amount of time (i.e., the user cannot extend their time indefinitely, but in set two-hour blocks). The administrator in this case is an automated system that revalidates the user credentials for each two-hour block and allows work to continue. This whole process is logged as well and can be reviewed later if required due to an audit or an incident postmortem.

Zero Trust for Third-Party Applications at KC Enterprises

Most organizations trust applications too explicitly, and that was found to be the case in KC Enterprises as well. Most third-party applications received little to no testing or integrity checks and had loose enforcement around service accounts and virtually no scanning of the workloads. As the tagging of any resource or workload progressed, any application or workload identified as third party was appropriately labeled in the relevant SoR (primarily the CMDB). Additionally, some applications had records in the VMS that were linked through APIs. This allowed the team to then take an inventory and begin to take a risk-based approach to this effort. For example, not all third-party applications present the same level of risk. Identifying those vendor applications or workloads that are higher risk (money-movement software, the applications supporting and running in the trusted zone) allowed the project team to focus on priority order and not get overwhelmed with the huge array of vendor applications. Many organizations rely on third-party applications, services, and workloads to operate a large part of their business, and KC was no exception. KC is designed to make widgets, not software. It might make software to help sell its product, but it is not going to make word processing, money-transaction software, or network operating systems. Those will always be outsourced, but not all of them present at the same risk level to KC Enterprises.

Third-Party Application Development and Workload Integrity In this space, the team dealt with the service and DevOps accounts issues, as they were seen as different from a normal user account. Service and DevOps accounts often have elevated privileges and require more controls as a result.

A number of vendors supplied services for development of software: The makers of the customer database, the HR software, and the KC product sizer were all required to be able to log in to KC network to access those systems for collaborative work with the business owners. Prior to the changes, there were no controls to ensure developers had segregated access levels (different accounts) to access development databases versus production databases. The changes now required separate accounts for each level of environment, and the duration for which these accounts could remain in specific environments was restricted, with shorter durations imposed on higher-risk environments. Developers are now required to not only have MFA for access, but their requirements for complexity also increased along with the requirement to use the PAM tool to manage passwords. This system integrated with the Active Directory to ensure passwords were rotated more frequently per the policy and context of location in the network.

Service accounts were handled slightly differently in that they could not always be federated and as a result were allowed to be accounts within the KC Active Directory. However, a lot of additional controls and processes were added to ensure they conformed with ZT goals. First, service accounts were required to meet all existing requirements for complexity, duration, history, etc. And where possible (and highly encouraged), the requirement is to have the service accounts managed by the PAM systems to further reduce the chance of a service account being compromised. When a service account cannot be integrated into the PAM solution, it is tagged in the Active Directory and other SoRs as required as non-PAM managed. However, the service account must still meet the minimum standards for service accounts.

Third-Party Application Least-Privileged Access Workload to Workload   There were a number of instances discovered in the earlier phases of the project where different vendor applications were "talking" to other vendors or KC Enterprises applications or products. Just as KC was overtrusting of applications, it was found that there was little thought given as to how the security was done in this interaction between workloads. Some of this risk was reduced by controlling the service accounts better with tooling and process. In addition, there was a need for a process and detective controls to be in place when a request originated from a vendor workload to access any other workload. First the process was changed to require an ARB review and approval for any connectivity between services or applications. Second, there were requirements on the access allowed between them to ensure it was confined to least privilege and not defaulted to root level access for the ease of the administrator or the workload itself. As the connectivity request was evaluated, the question of what level of access was reviewed and vetted. Detective controls were set up to find this communication and determine whether it was potentially malicious.

Third-Party Application Scanning   As mentioned earlier, the detective controls in this space were increased due to an earlier overtrusting approach. The logging and monitoring for all these resources and activities were increased and more widely shared across the various tools (SIEM, DLP, etc.) to allow for the context-driven decisions on access and data movement. The triggers for when the teammates engaged in these activities was lower than normal users, given the increased risk from these types of users. Again, this monitoring process underlays all three rows in the OSI model, allowing for ongoing threat hunting within the environment and facilitating improvements as issues are discovered. The project team continued to integrate the logging and system records into the SIEM, DLP, IDS/IPS systems to drive the context decisions.

Zero Trust for Third-Party Infrastructure at KC Enterprises

Infrastructure plays a big part in any organization that uses technology, and KC Enterprises found many areas and opportunities to improve their security for third parties in this domain. Factors critical to ZT success include how vendors access the infrastructure, identifying third-party devices, and ensuring they all have least-privilege access and are all part of the scanning process.

Third-Party User Access to Infrastructure   Vendors often need access to their equipment, whether physical or logical access. Physical access to KC systems was not integrated before, so the team took a bit of time integrating all the physical access control systems at the main office and all remote offices. This would allow for a central authority to ensure physical access matched the context-driven decisions, similar to how they were made when requesting logical access to a resource. Before this change, a vendor would have to make separate requests to access the same equipment in two separate locations. This lack of integration also meant there was no way to integrate the activity in each instance. When a vendor was offboarded, it was a challenge to go and find out each physical location they had access to and remove them individually. Combining the access to buildings and areas within those buildings allowed for more granular, context decisions about where and when a third-party had physical access to any location at KC Enterprises. The policy engine behind the physical access systems would ensure only the doors and areas required to perform their operation were opened.

Third-Party Device Integrity   There was already a discussion in the first row for third-party users about checking user and device integrity, but the focus there was mainly on users. In this pillar, the project team focused like a laser on any hardware device attached to the network; from networking equipment to Internet of Things (IoT) devices, they were an area of concern and focus. NAC was enabled and required for any and all connections to the KC network, but it was discovered that some devices could not support 802.1x. The decision was to not force them off the network immediately, but instead that all devices must support that protocol no later than one year from the standard being updated to require 802.1x.

The NAC database was integrated with the CMDB to ensure any items allowed on the network were included or added (as new ones connected and were approved). The tagging of third-party devices was a requirement as the devices were cataloged and connected. This tagging went to the heart of the monitoring and scanning requirements on all third-party devices.

Third-Party Infrastructure Segmentation   Segmentation of the network was a requirement and principle of ZT. The infrastructure requirements for this change were an upgrade to the firewalls and how the network and network security teams manage the network. As the tags on traffic identified it as third-party and assuming the traffic met the conditions for access at the NGFW, the network would place all vendor traffic on a separate VLAN. This VLAN allowed that traffic to be confined to that specific virtual LAN segment as it traversed the network. In some cases, this VLAN was not allowed into areas where there was no need for a vendor to perform business. For example, it was determined that the intellectual property database would never have a third-party access. The one use case where access to

IP data would be needed, to the patent attorneys, will not be by access to the database but via a legal document sent to them or details conveyed to them through deposition or artifacts. IoT devices were placed on another VLAN due to the view from KC cyber team that these devices were an increased risk compared to other infrastructure. This VLAN ensured that any IoT device was isolated on this segment.

Segmentation not only applied horizontally but also vertically within the network. Prior to the changes, the network was extremely flat in comparison to the desired outcome for ZT. Notice the delineation in the network for trusted zone as the most obvious segmentation from the enterprise network. The segmentation was also for the access to cloud instances. The team severed the direct connections to KC's AWS cloud SaaS application, which served as a front end for the customer database. Third-party users who would connect to this website (or a customer) would have their access granted based on the context of the user, and not just via an open pipe back to the customer database.

Third-Party Infrastructure Scanning Scanning of all infrastructure across the appropriate VLANs was the final step of monitoring the enterprise for third-party malicious activity. Because they had placed all network infrastructure and IoT devices on separate VLANs, the monitoring tools and processes could focus narrowly. The activity in this space is fairly easy to baseline, meaning that most infrastructure or workloads behave largely the same way at the same times as opposed to users who can be a bit more unpredictable. This allowed for a narrower band of thresholds for these activities before an alert of anomalous behavior makes its way to a human for review (or an automated reaction based on the ruleset).

Written Policy Changes

The project team was charged with updating a number of written policy changes. First was the overall information security program document. This document describes the scope and intent of the cybersecurity team and its leadership. Then the team reviewed a number of other documents, from standards and policies, to the secondary and tertiary documents such as security baselines, process, runbooks, and procedures. The changes were not confined to cybersecurity; they branched out into technology (network, users' access) as well as documentation dealing with third parties, such as the TPRM policy, the supplier management policy, and legal policies and processes.

Identity and Access Management Program

Identity is a key pillar in any ZT deployment. There were required changes to the IAM program and policies for this project. First the team had to add language in the IAM standard that stated "All third-parties are required to have a multifactor authentication for logging in to any KC Enterprises system or network." However, there was a step just prior to this first step: determining how many and/or which vendors will be challenged to utilize an MFA process where the application or service is not designed for it. The first step in this process was to take the inventory of all third-party applications or systems that require a vendor to log in and inquire if the application or service is designed and/or set up for MFA. There were two applications discovered that due to their design and age were not able to natively support MFA. For these two applications, for the short term they were placed within a VDI that required a one-time token along with their username and password to access. Longer term, the team worked with the vendor to redesign the applications for MFA support.

The requirement to have third-party user and service accounts be "continuously monitored" was added to the IAM standard along with that any user or service also must meet any "configuration and security profiles" prior to connecting. The term *continuously monitored* in this case meant that user and service accounts were not just checked at time of initial access requests but also at intervals during their connectivity that were determined by their risk levels. This also used user-behavior tools and processes to look for anomalous activity by a third-party user or service.

Vulnerability Management Program

There were a number of third-party applications and products running in KC Enterprises that it was discovered were not being inventoried or monitored. This meant that a large risk area was not being managed by the vulnerability management program. The root cause for this was a lack of awareness on many parts of the organization. First, the lines of business would "add" items of risk to an engagement over the life of a relationship organically. It wasn't that the business leadership was complacent about security, but as there were new capabilities requested or required, they were almost always approved due a flaw in the design of the approval process.

When a vendor requested a new connectivity option and had no prior relationship with KC Enterprises, a review of the connectivity and risk were required. This was part of normal intake in TPRM, which included asking risk-related questions and conducting a cyber evaluation based on the connection requirement. In the case of a third party with an existing relationship, if the vendor went through a cyber evaluation previously, the workflow tool for the connection request did not check whether that particular connectivity had been assessed in the previous evaluation. Other examples of additional risk that grew organically and undetected were increases in data sensitivity that went unreported. Within the vulnerability management program at KC was the DLP team, whose job it is to understand where risks lie. Some of this is done with detective controls, but an inventory of where sensitive data is shared is both a policy and regulatory-driven requirement.

The changes required in this space were to focus on ensuring the program documentation and process runbooks all contained specific language for TPR identification and monitoring. As previously stated, the business side lacked knowledge when assessing risks, which resulted in other teams responsible for those risks being unaware of the significant risk that was accumulating. This lack of awareness extended to both the vendor and enterprise levels, leading to a lack of reporting or accountability for this unaddressed risk.

Cybersecurity Incident Management Program

The JR Software incident exposed some challenges in how incident management was conducted at KC Enterprises. Although the cyber incident management team (CIMT) is responsible for handling all incidents within the organization, their focus and documentation was primarily on incidents directly involving KC Enterprises, and not so much on third or fourth parties. The process was ad hoc for third-party or fourth-party incidents and required a more formally documented and rehearsed process. The first changes to the documentation were at the program level on incidents that described the process for when a third or fourth party is potentially affected by a cyber incident, breach, or event. The team designed a workflow to follow and also designed a runbook for the process. Secondly, the process for including the cyber third-party risk (CTPR) team was designed primarily for use during normal business hours. This was not working the night the JR Software incident occurred, given it was at the end of the day Friday. The CTPR team taught the CIMT teammates how to perform the third-party information lookups in the SoRs and also shared the runbook for the same process. Further, there was a scenario for third- or fourth-party incidents required in any tabletop exercise going forward at KC Enterprises. This ensured the teams practiced this important handoff and got it smooth when it counted.

Cybersecurity Program

At the cybersecurity program, the information security program document had seven main parts: Introduction, Objectives, Responsibilities, Program Description, Program Owners, Glossary, and Version Control. Updates to the document were focused on explaining this new approach to ZT in appropriate locations. In the Objectives section, there was an additional bullet added: "Ensure that all high-value assets are protected by zero-trust principles such as least-privilege access, microsegmentation, and protecting the critical assets as defined by business and cybersecurity." In the Program Description section, additional wording was added around some of the specifics required for ZT in the program. For example, the Manage and Control Risks part of this section added the wording on least privilege and microsegmentation specifics in these headings: Access Controls, Application Security, Network Security, Data Loss Prevention, Firewalls and Intrusion Detection, and Incident Response.

Cybersecurity Third-Party Risk Program

Under the CISO, the TPR team in cybersecurity was reporting to the leader of the cyber vulnerability management team. After this series of events and the raising of the profile and importance of third-party risk to KC Enterprises, the decision was made for this team to report directly to the CISO and elevate the leadership role with a more senior leader. The intent in this shift is to ensure the third-party risk team has a direct path into the cyber senior leadership. This team would be responsible for maintaining and monitoring the ZT deployments at KC Enterprises and reporting on key performance indicators (KPIs) and key risk indicators (KRIs). Maria, the CISO, strategized that the team required an up-leveling to help make this happen.

The next changes to the cybersecurity program for third-party risk was to make it more attuned to the ZT policy and principal changes. In the overarching Cybersecurity Third-Party Risk Program document, which includes the objectives, responsible parties, summary of capabilities, glossary, and version control, the team added language about ZT principles and policies being a guide for how this program is executed at KC Enterprises. The team set about adding least privilege, assume a breach, and trust no one into the document where appropriate. They also added language to align with the TPRM program on their risk-based approach. This focused on taxonomy and how they were categorized:

- **Systemically critical:** These are vendors that at the enterprise level if they were unavailable would prevent KC Enterprises from completing normal business operations.
- **Business critical:** These are vendors that are systemically critical for a specific line of business, but not the entire company.
- **High risk:** These are vendors with more than 1M customer records or a connection to the KC networks. A few additional criteria can land a vendor in this category:

- Any vendor with a breach in the past three years
- Any vendor with more than two high-risk cyber findings
- Management discretion

- **Medium risk:** These are vendors with between 250,000 and 1M customer records.
- **Low risk:** These are vendors with fewer than 250,000 customer records.

After this, the team addressed several more things: the third-party security standard, the information security addendum, and assessment alignment and due diligence, which are discussed in more detail next.

Third-Party Security Standard

The third-party security standard, which is managed and owned by the TPR team within cybersecurity, required updates to accommodate the ZT journey. A *third-party security standard* is an internal document that describes what KC Enterprises holds its vendors and third-parties to in terms of cyber controls. It is not shared with the vendors, but instead is designed to inform teammates at KC and is accessible through the policy document SoR.

Updates to the standard were focused on the main areas of ZT policy and control changes. Some of the changes were conditional; for example, if the vendor does not make software, then any controls for that space would be considered not applicable. In addition, not all vendors were subject to this level of controls: Low-risk vendors, by definition, are low risk to KC and this level of oversight would be overkill. These controls were considered applicable when a vendor hit the high risk or above. The model was based upon the Cybersecurity and Infrastructure Security Agency (CISA) Zero Trust Maturity Model from April 2023.

This model shows four different maturity models for ZT deployment. traditional, initial, advanced, and optimal. It was determined that low-risk and medium-risk vendors can adhere to the basic level laid out, while high risk must be in the advanced level for ZT, and the business and systemically critical vendors must adhere to the optimal level of ZT deployment. Following are the questions to ask a vendor to determine their level of maturity on ZT per the CISA model:

- **Access controls**
  - Vendor shall have a privileged access management process/system.
  - Vendor shall require privileged access users or users with elevated permissions to be managed by the privileged access management system.
  - Vendor must log all access control activity and forward that log to a SIEM or similar system for analysis.
  - Vendor will ensure all devices connecting to the network are checked for security posture and allowed access to the network.
  - Vendor will perform continuous validation of users and devices on the network.
  - Vendor shall have visibility, analytics, and orchestration process, tools, and systems for best-practices governance.
  - Vendor authenticates on first-time access and at least once every hour until access is terminated.
  - Vendor shall have some federation of identity with cloud and on-premises systems when appropriate.
  - Vendor will determine identity risk based on rules and analytics.
  - Vendor has a centralized user visibility system.
  - Vendor has a policy-based automated access revocation process.

- **Network controls**
  - Vendor will have defined micro-perimeters for egress and ingress points.
  - All traffic is encrypted in transit, regardless of location in network.
  - Vendor will have a system or process to analyze network traffic for anomalous behavior.
  - Vendor shall have visibility, analytics, and orchestration process, tools, and systems for best-practices governance.
  - Vendor will have a NAC or 802.1x system deployed that is centrally managed.
  - Vendor uses automated workflows to initiate network and environmental changes.
  - Vendor has automated discovery of networks, devices, and services.
  - Vendor uses user-based routing to support network access control.

- **Assets and devices**
  - Vendor shall have compliance enforcement for any device connecting to the network.
  - Vendor shall assess access to data on first-time access and at least every hour while device is connected.
  - Vendor uses automated methods to manage assets.
  - Vendor uses automated methods to identify vulnerabilities and patching.
  - Vendor reconciles device inventory against a list of non-compliant devices.
  - Vendor provisions devices using automated, repeatable methods.
  - Vendor devices adhere to best practices for supporting security functions in hardware.

- **Application security**
  - Vendor shall have a centralized authentication, authorization, monitoring, and attributes for application access.
  - Vendor will have integration of threat protections for application workflows.
  - Vendor cloud applications and on-premises applications are accessible over Internet or VPN.
  - Vendor integrates application testing into application development and deployment practices with dynamic testing.
  - Vendor performs application health and security monitoring on a continuous basis.
  - Vendor has ability to alert when device and network components of application changing state.
  - Vendor has policies and enforcement centralized.
  - Vendor uses policy-based access for ephemeral identities.

- **Data security**
  - Vendor continuously monitors inventory of data with tagging and tracking.
  - Vendor governs access to data using least-privilege controls that consider identity, device risk, and other attributes.
  - Vendor encrypts all data at rest.
  - Vendor ensures all data in lower environments is anonymized and contains no production or sensitive data.
  - Vendor's data is inventoried on a continuous basis.
  - Vendor logs and analyzes all access events to data for suspect behavior.
  - Vendor enforces strict access controls automatically for sensitive or high-risk data.
  - Vendor data policies drive policy enforcement.
  - Vendor has defined data access governance to support data security.

Information Security Addendum   The updates next up were to the information security addendum. This document was broken into two parts to allow for easier negotiations. The first part is the legal wording required in the addendum. This was updated and is described in the "Legal Policies" section later in this chapter. The second part is a clarification of controls, as expected, and tied to NIST-CSF to ensure most cyber organizations can align requirements with their own framework. Although many companies use NIST-CSF in their cyber framework, some do not. However, if the vendor uses another framework, it is possible for them to translate that because most of them "borrow" from each other. The following sections discuss the updates to the controls in the information security addendum related to NIST-CSF subdomains.

Cloud Security   The team updated the controls for the Cloud Security NIST subdomain (NIST references CSA, CISA):

- Third parties must agree to provide independent verification (e.g., federal risk and authorization management level medium, CSA certification for cloud deployments, HiTrust, SOC 2 Type II, etc.) in place of a full security assessment, should KC Enterprises request this.

Business Continuity   The team updated the controls for the Business Continuity NIST subdomain (NIST references ID SC-5, PR.IP-4, PR.IP-9, PR.IP-10, PR.PT-5, RS.MI-1, RS.MI-2, RC.RP-1):

- Third party must automatically and on a regular basis, perform complete, comprehensive, and resilient backups of (i) KC Enterprises' sensitive data in custody or control, and

(ii) systems and information necessary to the performance and availability of the services (such as system data needed to operate systems).

- KC Enterprises' restricted information as well as systems and information necessary for the performance and availability of the services must be backed up at least daily.

- Third party shall segregate backups from production environments and maintain them in a manner that is resilient to physical disaster and malicious attack (e.g., ransomware), including using encryption and ensuring that backups have at least one offline backup destination (i.e., not accessible via a network connection).

- Third party shall conduct regular testing of backup restoration and shall implement a plan to ensure rapid and successful recovery of data in the event of a disruption to the performance or availability of the services resulting from a system outage or security incident.

PCI/Payment Card   The team updated the controls for the PCI/ Payment Card NIST subdomain (NIST references for PCI standards):

- As applicable, third party must comply with PCI security standards (i.e., PCI PTS, PCI PA-DSS, PCI DSS, PCI, P2PE), as well as obtain and maintain applicable third-party PCI security standards certification.

- Third party is responsible for the security of KC Enterprises' cardholder data that third party possesses or otherwise stores, processes, or transmits on behalf of third party and will furnish evidence of current PCI security standards certification for the relevant services.

- Third party will conduct PCI security standards required quarterly network scans on the in-scope environment via an approved scanning third party (as defined by PCI security standards), whose use is hereby consented to by KC Enterprises.

- To the extent that third party is performing services that are "in scope" of Payment Card Industry standards (PCI service provider or merchants) and acting on behalf of KC Enterprises, third party must have their PCI scope assessed by a qualified security assessor (QSA) with an annual report of compliance (ROC).

- Third party shall provide, upon request and on a defined rolling basis, evidence of compliance (i.e., an attestation of compliance, certificate of compliance, etc.).

Data Destruction   The team updated the controls for the Data Destruction NIST subdomain (NIST references PR.DS-3, PR.IP-6):

- Third parties must agree to return or securely dispose of KC Enterprises' information assets upon termination of the third-party relationship.

- Third party must provide evidence (e.g., certificate of destruction) of data destruction in line with termination of vendor relationship with KC Enterprises and/or in line with retention policies as previously agreed upon.

Physical Security   The team updated the controls for the Physical Security NIST subdomain (NIST references PR.AC-2, PR.DS-8, PR.IP-7, DE.AE-1, DE.CM-1, DE.CM-2, DE.CM-3):

- Physical security requirements, controls, and measures must be in place for KC Enterprises assets at third-party facilities.

- Third party must implement and maintain administrative, physical, and technical safeguards designed to protect KC Enterprises' sensitive data and covered third-party systems from unauthorized access, acquisition, disclosure, destruction, alteration, unavailability, misuse, or damage, which must meet or exceed relevant and currently accepted industry standards, including but not limited to the NIST Cybersecurity Framework, the International Organization for Standardization (ISO) 27001/2 Series of Standards, and the Control Objectives for Information and related Technology (COBIT) Standards.

- Any third-party personnel who accesses any KC Enterprises' system or any facility of KC Enterprises or one of its affiliates during or in connection with performance of services must comply with KC Enterprises' information security and physical security policies and procedures.

Awareness and Training   The team updated the controls for the Awareness and Training NIST subdomain (NIST references PR.AT-1, PR.IR-11):

- Third party must provide information security awareness training at least annually to all its personnel with access to KC Enterprises' sensitive data or KC Enterprises' systems that materially covers the security requirements of this baseline and must include phishing training.

Software Security   The team updated the controls for the Software Security NIST subdomain (NIST references PR.DS-87, PR.IP-2, PR.IP-3):

- Third party must implement appropriate technical and organization measures to ensure the delivery of secure code (e.g., the OWASP Application Security Verification Standard), including strong configuration management, application security testing, runtime exploit prevention, and no vulnerable open source code.

- Third party's development will not be complete until the security of the code and application has been demonstrated via a security report. Such security report must be provided by third party and reviewed and accepted by KC Enterprises.

- Third party must not store, transmit, access, or display any production data within nonproduction systems designated as development, quality assurance, or test.

- Third party must have a secure software development policy that applies to all development practices.

- Third party must have operationalized procedures to manage and verify secure development, deployment, and maintenance of applications.

- KC Enterprises must reserve the right to test (including dynamic application security testing [DAST], static application security testing [SAST], and penetration testing [PEN]) all third-party software used in connection with the services. When not feasible, third party must, at its own expense, provide to KC Enterprises an independent verification of test execution, results, and remediation plans where applicable.

- Prior to delivery, third-party software must not have an open CVE with a CVSS of 8.0 or higher in score, based on the then-current CVSS version.

- Third party must notify KC Enterprises within 24 hours when third party becomes aware of any zero-day vulnerabilities in software they provide.

- For any third party providing software that meets the definition of critical software, third party will provide these additional security controls:

  - Third party must provide a software bill of materials (BOM) that will describe at a minimum:
    - List of all open source and third-party components
    - License for open source and third-party components
    - Versions and patch status for open source and third-party components

  - Third party must provide a method to authenticate their software that is immutable, such as code signing.

Web Applications   The team updated the controls for the Web Applications NIST subdomain (NIST references ID.RA-1, ID.RA-3, PR.DS-5, DE.CM-6, DE.CM-8):

- Third party must use industry standard tuned and configured web application firewall (WAF) or similar technology that is designed to protect known injection attacks, broken authentication, sensitive data exposure, XML external entities (XXE), broken access control, security misconfigurations, cross-site scripting (XSS), and insecure deserialization, or other technologies that provide similar web application security at runtime.

- Prior to implementation, WAF must be scanned and remediated using accepted industry standard tools for security vulnerabilities (e.g., Open Web Application Security Project and Open Web Application Security Project Top 10).

- WAF must be scanned for vulnerabilities and vulnerabilities must be promptly remediated. Scanning must be at a frequency that is appropriate for the relevant application, technology, and data risk.

- External-facing websites maintained by a third party on behalf of KC Enterprises must be configured with the following account and password controls and must meet the full set of requirements set forth in the most updated version of National Institute of Standards and Technology (NIST) SP 800-63B-3 and SP 800-63-3, or alternatively, the following minimum set of requirements:

  - Password complexity must be implemented for all accounts
  - Complexity must include at least three of the four: one uppercase, one lowercase, one special character, and one number
  - Periodic forced password changes no more than every ninety (90) calendar days
  - Account lockout after no more than ten (10) failed attempts in 30 minutes
  - Prohibit group or shared accounts/passwords
  - Prohibit use of default passwords
  - Password history of at least 10 remembered
  - Minimum password age of one day

- Periodically check passwords against known password dictionaries
- Passwords should support all ASCII characters (spaces included)
- Passwords must not be shortened during processing
- External-facing websites must additionally implement and maintain accepted industry standard account and password management controls, including:
  - First-time and one-time password login expiration after no more than 24 hours
  - Prohibit user IDs, passwords, and personal data from being displayed in a URL
  - Store user passwords and reset/forgotten security questions in an encrypted manner
  - Reauthentication is required after no more than 15 minutes of inactivity
  - Prohibit the storage of passwords or personal data in persistent local storage (caches, etc.) or in any cookies, JavaScript, or other web tracking technology
- Applications hosted by a third party for KC Enterprises teammate login must be restricted to KC Enterprises' own networks unless otherwise specified in the terms of the contract.

Network Security   The team updated the controls for the Network Security NIST subdomain (NIST references PR.PT-4, PR.AC-5, PR.DS-2, DE.CM-1):

- Third-party networks must be managed, monitored, and controlled to protect KC Enterprises' sensitive data.

- Third party shall implement multilayered network security infrastructure that provides continuous monitoring, restricts unauthorized network traffic, and detects and limits the impact of attacks, including: (i) firewalls or other filtering devices, and (ii) intrusion detection systems (IDS) and/or intrusion prevention systems (IPS) configured and maintained to ensure optimal protection, log suspicious or unauthorized network traffic patterns, and to alert third-party personnel of actual or suspected compromises.

- Network traffic shall be appropriately segregated with routing and access controls separating traffic on internal networks from public or other untrusted networks.

- High-risk administrative ports (e.g., Telnet) and ports on external-facing systems that are not required for business functions should not be accessible from the Internet.

- Information systems, network devices, and applications shall be configured and deployed using a secure baseline (hardened), maintained to address known vulnerabilities, and with extraneous ports/services disabled.

- Third party shall restrict the connection times of idle/inactive sessions on information systems, applications, and network devices, and terminate inactive sessions.

- If the third party has a connection to a KC Enterprises' network (intermittent or static) where the third-party's equipment is used to enable the connectivity, the third party shall biannually attest that the connectivity equipment is updated and patched according to their own internal process and procedures.

- Out-of-band communications (OOB). If the third party requires out-of-band communications to manage their equipment and/or software, they must ensure one or more of the following:

- **Dialback**: When management access is required, the user dials the number associated with the device. The device answers, hangs up, and then calls a preconfigured number.
- **Caller ID**: Only calls from specific, predefined phone numbers accepted.
- **Secure modem**: Each of the connections requires a specific, preconfigured modem.
- **Touchtone password device**: Such an inline device requires a distinct password to be entered using touchtone numbers.
- **Access management for OOB**: All access transactions, whether successful or not, should be logged to a separate logging facility. Any unsuccessful access should cause an immediate alert to be generated and forwarded to a real-time (or as close to real-time as practical) monitoring system. This system can range from a console display at a 24x7 staffed operations center to email or pager notification. Assessment logs should be reviewed on a regular basis.

Virus and Malware   The team updated the controls for the Virus and Malware NIST subdomain (NIST references PR.DS-8, ID.RA-1, ID.RA-3, DE.CM-4, DE.CM-5, DE.CM-8):

- Third party must have antivirus/malware protection enabled on all servers and workstations that access, process, or store KC Enterprises' proprietary information.
- Third-party antivirus/malware tools must use centrally managed virus signature updates updated at least daily.
- Third-party antivirus/malware tools must periodically perform endpoint scans and promptly remediate any findings.

- Third-party work product that is intended to be installed on KC Enterprises' systems must not contain mechanisms that will harm KC Enterprises' systems, cause KC Enterprises' systems to become inaccessible to KC enterprises, or permit any third party to access KC Enterprises' proprietary information or systems.

- Third party must ensure that its and third-party personnel's vulnerability patch processes and procedures are designed and implemented to industry best practices or as specified in InfoSec addendum.

Access Controls   The team updated the controls for the Access Controls NIST subdomain (NIST references PR.AC-3, PR.AC-4, PR.AC-7, PR.PT-1, DE.AE-2, DE.AE-3, PR.PT-4, PR.DS-5, ID.RA-4, ID.RA-5):

- Third party must restrict access to KC Enterprises' systems and KC Enterprises' sensitive data to a need basis using the principle of least privilege. Unless otherwise specifically approved in a statement of work (SOW), third-party must maintain the KC Enterprises' operating environment (including any KC Enterprises' sensitive data) in a segregated state from third-party internal environments and those environments used by/for third-party's other clients such that only authorized third-party personnel or subcontractors providing services to KC Enterprises may gain access.

- All remote access by third-party personnel is subject to written approval from KC Enterprises prior to accessing KC Enterprises' systems and KC Enterprises' sensitive data. Such approval may be either in the form of a duly executed SOW or from a KC Enterprises' senior vice president (or the current equivalent title) or above at the time of remote-access invocation. In the event of a pandemic or other such disaster-recovery event, third party must provide a weekly remote access personnel status report to KC Enterprises for all third-party personnel connecting to KC Enterprises' systems.

- Third party must use two-factor authentication for (i) all accounts with privileged or elevated access rights to systems or applications hosting or processing KC Enterprises' sensitive data, and (ii) any remote access by third party to systems or KC Enterprises' sensitive data.

- Third party must perform adequate logging and monitoring of access-related activities; access to these logs should be reviewed and restricted to only those personnel that have a need to know.

- Third party must collect and evaluate security events using appropriate tools, including an effective security information and event management (SIEM) system.

- Third-party personnel are required to use a KC Enterprises' or third-party-controlled device when accessing KC Enterprises' systems and KC Enterprises' sensitive data.

- Third-party-controlled devices must be continuously monitored when accessing KC Enterprises' systems and KC Enterprises' sensitive data.

- No KC Enterprises' data may be copied to or stored in a third-party device unless previously approved in a SOW.

- Third-party devices must be hardened in accordance with the Level 1 Center for Internet Security Benchmark profile and controlled via group policy objects.

- Third-party devices shall have a mandatory login, screen inactivity/locking timeout (fifteen (15) minutes).

- Third-party virtual private network (VPN) shall be configured to be "always on." If not technically feasible, each hardened device shall have On and Off Net Proxy with a reasonable level of controls (i.e., content filtering).

- VPN software must be installed utilizing NIST-approved cryptographic schemes and algorithms with at least 2048-bit and/or 256-bit encryption as applicable.

- When connecting to the KC Enterprises' network, third-party personnel must be limited through network capabilities (e.g., firewall, routing, etc.) to connect only to the designated KC Enterprises' environment. Split tunneling is prohibited.

- Third-party devices must have third-party-managed, commercial-grade data loss prevention control software designed and must be configured to prevent and detect data leaks of KC Enterprises' sensitive data on in-scope systems and networks.

- Any removable media (CD/DVD drive, USB port(s), etc.) must be adequately configured to prevent any storage device from connecting. In cases where a business requirement is determined that requires such connection, the third party must ensure the following:
  - An effective policy that covers such deviations is in place.
  - Deviations must be time-limited.
  - Deviations must be reviewed at least annually.
  - Deviations are documented and approved by the CISO or equivalent.
  - All controls protecting the connections from ingress/egress of data or malware are in place and effective.

- Third-party personnel remote access must be restricted to the United States, or to such other country locations identified and agreed to by KC Enterprises in the SOW or master service agreement.

Encryption and Data The team updated the controls for the Encryption and Data NIST subdomain (NIST references PR.DS-1, PR.DS-2, PR.DS-3, PR.PT-4):

- Third-party portable media and devices that contain KC Enterprises' sensitive data must be encrypted, using Advanced Encryption Standard (AES) 256-bit encryption or NIST-approved encryption algorithm; all key lengths must utilize 256-bit key length or greater.
- Third party must encrypt KC Enterprises' sensitive data in third party's control, at rest and in transit, using Advanced Encryption Standard (AES) 256-bit encryption or NIST-approved encryption algorithm; all key lengths must utilize 256-bit key length or greater.
- Third party must have effective encryption key management procedures.
- Third party must notify KC Enterprises of any reasonably suspected or actual compromise of any encryption key used to protect KC Enterprises' sensitive data.
- In cases where KC Enterprises' sensitive data is in a multi-tenant environment, encryption keys unique to KC Enterprises must be used, unless specifically authorized by KC Enterprises in either the contract or SOW.
- Encryption keys must be rotated every 24 months or less.

Personnel Onsite Access   The team updated the controls for the Personnel Onsite Access NIST subdomain (NIST references PR.DS-1, PR.DS-2, PR.DS-3, PR.PT-4, PR.AC-6, PR.AC-7, PR.AC-1, PR.AC-3, PR.AC-4, DE.AE-2, DE.AE-3):

- Third-party systems that access, process, or store KC Enterprises' sensitive information must be managed using the principle of least privilege.

- Password requirements are a full set of the requirements set by the most updated version of National Institute of Standards and Technology (NIST) SP 800-63B-3 and SP 800-63-3, or alternatively, the following set of requirements.

- Third-party user passwords must be at least ten (10) characters and contain at least three (3) different attributes from the following list:
  - Uppercase letters
  - Lowercase letters
  - Numbers
  - Special characters
  - Passwords should support ASCII characters (including spaces), must have a minimum age of one day, and not allow for dictionary words
  - User passwords must have a minimum age of one (1) day and must be changed at least every 90 days
  - User accounts must be locked out after no more than ten (10) failed attempts

- Third-party group or shared accounts/passwords are prohibited.

- Third party must not use default passwords.

- Two-factor authentication must be used for all third-party user accounts with privileged or elevated rights to Systems that host or process KC Sensitive Information.

- Two-factor authentication must be used for third-party user remote access to systems that host or process KC Sensitive Information.
- Third party must perform user access reviews at least twice annually.
- Third party must perform privileged user access reviews at least quarterly.
- Third party must have procedures in place for provisioning and deprovisioning third-party user access.
- Third party must log and monitor all access related activity:
  - All general user account access logs must be retained for a minimum of 90 days
  - All general user account access logs must be retained for a minimum of 12 months if Third Party employees will be accessing KC network.
  - All elevated privilege (Admin/System) account access logs must be retained for a minimum of 12 months.

Third-Party Management   The team updated the controls for the Third-Party Management NIST subdomain (NIST reference NIST 800-171):

- Third party will require all subcontractors who process, transmit, store, or access sensitive data to enter into a written agreement that commits the subcontractor to adhere to security requirements no less rigorous than those set forth in this exhibit.
- Third party must obtain additional written consent prior to permitting a subcontractor to process, transmit, store, or access sensitive data.

- Third party must maintain a list of all such subcontractors and furnish that list upon request.

- Third party must maintain an effective vendor management program to provide oversight on subcontractors engaged to provide services to KC Enterprises.

The Information Security Addendum Updates in Action   These updates to the information security addendum were made effective on the day of approval by the CISO and chief legal counsel for KC Enterprises. Then the team undertook an effort to get this update's terms and conditions into all systemically critical, business-critical, and then high-risk vendors at the organization. This was a multiyear effort because many of the vendors did not have renewal clauses (they were what are called *evergreen* agreements where, unless one of the parties raises their hand, the contracts were auto-renewed without any requirement for renegotiation). This team worked with both the TPRM leadership and legal team to place these vendors on a "watch list," which meant they could not renew or get new business until these terms were properly updated.

The team did run into some vendors who were "too big to care." These are companies that due to the lack of serious competition or their position (for example, SWIFT in banking is a required third party if the financial institute wants to conduct normal banking operations, but SWIFT will never let a customer perform any due diligence). These organizations act as near monopolies due to these circumstances, and so KC Enterprises was not able to get the terms they required from these third parties. However, the company could not do business without them or could not conceivably produce a similar product or service on their own. The way they dealt with these vendors was to declare a type of vendor classification called Special Third Parties. This category was designed to house these types of too-big-to-care vendors that KC can't do without but can't get the due diligence per normal process. This list of vendors, Special Third Parties, was taken to the Third-Party Risk Committee (a board-level committee) to transparently discuss and approve on a yearly basis. This allowed the risks and decisions to be discussed openly at an appropriate level and to be reviewed annually. Aside from the way to deal with this as a program issue, there still arises the ZT principles around these too-big-to-care vendors, and this may be accomplished (or the risk reduced significantly) by leveraging more controls and management around these types of vendors. For example, place their connections in an enclave or demilitarized zone (DMZ) to isolate only the traffic expected from this vendor's connectivity. Have a higher level of logging and monitoring oversight on them. Because this list of third parties should be small, the extra work to get them ZT (even if a "lite" version) is better than none at all.

Assessment Alignment and Due Diligence   The last updates to the Cybersecurity Third-Party Risk Program were how to align the assessments and due diligence performed to align with the updates to the risk categories:

- **Systemically critical**: These are vendors that at the enterprise level, if unavailable would prevent KC Enterprises from completing normal business operations.

- **Business critical**: These are vendors that are systemically critical for a specific line of business, but not the entire company.

- **High risk**: These are vendors with more than 1M customer records or a connection to the KC networks. A few additional criteria can land a vendor in this category:
  - Any vendor with a breach in the last three years
  - Any vendor with more than two high-risk cyber findings
  - Management discretion
- **Medium risk**: These are vendors with between 250,000 and 1M customer records.
- **Low risk**: These are vendors with fewer than 250,000 customer records.

Systemically critical vendors are all required to have an onsite, physical validation for cybersecurity controls at least once a year unless allowed by management. More about what *unless allowed by management* means in a moment, but the concept of requiring vendors to undergo physical validation at the company location(s) is based on the inherent risks associated with these third parties. This requirement is vital to ensure thorough investigation and scrutiny in accordance with the defined standards. Any vendor in this category that could or would not perform an onsite physical validation must meet the appropriate level of monopoly status in its space so that no other option is available, and their exception requires C-level approvals.

The previous "unless allowed by management" statement about whether a vendor requires the onsite physical validation annually can be overridden for great reasons. For example, a vendor is providing KC Enterprises with a SaaS product in AWS and the vendor allows a level of collaboration on security controls. They allow your team to get the API feed (read-only) from AWS Trusted Advisor Report when an expected control is changed. The vendor could inform your team (and theirs) with this API when the Boolean checkbox for MFA for Root Access is flipped to off (it is enabled by default in AWS). This level of trust and collaboration could lower the number of point-in-time due diligence efforts required.

Systemically critical vendors were also required to have embarked on a ZT journey of their own. Using the CISA Zero Trust Maturity Model to measure their progress, this was worked into the onsite physical validation due diligence exercises, so it wasn't a separate process for vendor and line of business. There was an effort to encourage vendors who get further along in their maturity model by lowering the frequency of the due diligence. A systemically critical vendor measured in the advanced stages of maturity for over 90 percent of the domains required an onsite only every other year, whereas a vendor with optimal maturity rating for 90 percent of their domains has to endure an onsite physical validation only every three years.

Business-critical vendors were only required to have a virtual (not onsite) physical validation, unless otherwise required due to risk. The *unless otherwise* here could be the vendor has had a breach in the past three years, which increases the risk of a secondary incident or breach. A virtual physical validation was performed using any standard collaboration tools that all KC Enterprises and vendors got used to working with seamlessly during COVID lockdowns. This allows due diligence to continue with an important capability such as physical validation, but does not require the expense and work required for an onsite. Business-critical vendors were not required to have a ZT journey started, but were rewarded if they submitted proof they were at some maturity stage that could be physically validated. Typically, this tier of risk requires an annual physical validation due diligence be performed, but if the vendor can prove they are at

90 percent coverage for an advanced maturity rating on the CISA tables, they require an assessment only every other year. If they can prove they are at 90 percent for optimal rating, the due diligence cadence is lowered to every three years. This saves costs for both teams and increases the trust levels tremendously for KC Enterprises and vendors.

High-risk vendors did not require a physical validation of any type unless management decided the vendor meets certain criteria. Management discretion was similar to other risk levels: if a vendor had a breach in the last three years or was continually deficient on due diligence assessments to a degree that raised the risk significantly of a breach or incident. These vendors typically got the remote assessment questionnaires, where they typed in the responses. KC Enterprises wants to focus on these, but much less than the top two categories. This is partly a resource decision, but also a focus decision. Resources are a concern because at some point the team can't keep adding them. Focus is a concern for planning because even with enough resources, if the field is too wide it can be hard to focus on what is really important. The approach for this risk level was to automate as much as possible with artificial intelligence (AI) and machine learning (ML) tools to provide coverage on the mundane work of checking for compliance in questionnaires and only getting a human involved when the risk warrants it.

Medium and low risk were farmed out by KC Enterprises. In this case, it was decided to contract with a local accounting firm to train them on some abbreviated cyber and other risk domain checks. This team would perform all the required assessments per KC policy per a fixed price that provided a savings to the overall enterprise as the accounting firm offshored the work. None of this work was customer facing and mainly consisted of using AI and ML along with data feeds from KC Enterprise's previous due diligence to escalate only when thresholds were met.

Third-Party Risk Management Program

The TPRM team is the owner of the TPR program and standards and acts as second line for the supplier management team. Each of the risk domains (cybersecurity, financial, privacy, compliance, business continuity, fourth party, and legal) perform the due diligence and due care for their respective domains and provide TPRM with their risk evaluations. Any risks are identified as gaps and, depending on where the vendor is in the overall process (intake assessments or ongoing monitoring), are then stored in the SoR with a remediation plan or a risk acceptance.

TPRM changes were primarily focused on policy changes required to support the needs for a ZT journey in TPR. The first step was to better identify vendor risk types. Prior to the JR Software incident, the policy stated there were three categories: high, medium, and low risk. High was any vendor with more than 1M records or connection to KC Enterprises' networks. Medium was any vendor with more than 250,000 records to less than 999,999. Low risk was any vendor with 249,999 records or less. Because JR Software was so critical to the daily operations at KC Enterprises, the team needed to come up with a better way to focus on those third parties. There were two new designations made: systemically critical and business critical. *Systemically critical* are vendors that the whole company, KC Enterprises, requires to operate as a business. If one of these third parties goes offline, as did JR Software, the company would, at best, struggle to keep operations going. *Business critical* are vendors required to operate a specific line of business but not the whole company. For example, the finance department, under the chief financial officer (CFO), has listed one of their business-critical services as the vendor that does "daily close." This is a financial operation done daily to essentially wrap up the monetary transactions from each day. This third party is not essential to the sales team or the marketing team, but they also have their own business-critical services or products that would not affect finance if not working either.

The process to determine systemically critical and business critical is important, and Jimmy, as the project manager for the overall effort, was determined not to have scope creep. *Scope creep* is a project management term that refers to the original scope of a project slowly shifting over time without formal process to review and approve. In this case, the concern was the definitions of *systemically critical* and *business critical* would be too broad and cause a lot of third and fourth parties to be included in these lists. The decision was made that each vendor added to this list, either at the systemically critical or business-critical lists, would have to be "defended" to the Third-Party Risk Committee to ensure the list stayed focused and as short as possible.

Legal Policies

The primary changes in this area were centered around a specific project that received funding and had a designated project manager. The main objective was to review all third-party contracts to ensure all had appropriate language for incident notification and ZT principles were appropriate. In the JR Software incident, there was no incident notification or response language in their contracts. Subsequent to this discovery, the internal audit team dove into the records for all the third parties that would require this language and found nearly 80 percent had some material deficiencies in contract language. This ranged from not having incident notification to not having the appropriate terms and conditions language for cybersecurity/privacy. This effort was a multiyear effort, given the number of vendors, but the focus for the first year was on the critical vendors identified as part of the ZT journey.

Forcing a vendor to renegotiate a contract when it is not up for renewal is a challenge, so the legal team worked with the TPRM leadership to provide some "incentives" for them to come to the table. First, where the vendor was within a year of renewal, the legal team started the negotiations as many times as necessary to agree on terms. For third parties with longer durations left on their agreements, the TPRM placed them on a "restricted" list, thus preventing a vendor from renewing or getting new business until whatever put them on this list was resolved. Usually this was reserved for those third parties who had large risks or important missing information that rose to the level for a restricted list placement. However, its use isn't restricted to those circumstances, and preventing a vendor from renewing or gaining new business worked like a charm. Most organizations find that a large percentage of their vendors' activity in the sourcing process is existing vendors expanding existing business or renewing work. Although this didn't make vendors or their vendor managers internally at KC Enterprises very happy, it was effective at getting these folks to the table to negotiate to get terms the KC legal team was pursuing. The goal was to get incident response language in all critical vendor's contracts at 24 hours, with a fallback of 48 hours when a vendor would not agree to 24 hours' notice. In cases where the vendors would not agree to incident notice language, the policy was to not allow for those vendors to be accepted anymore when they meet requirements for incident notice. If a vendor would agree to notice but not adhere to anything 48 hours or less, this required escalation to both the line of business owner(s) as well as the CISO and chief counsel. This made it "expensive" in terms of time and effort to get these approved and hopefully discourage it being used.

Next were the updates required to the information security addendum. This document was broken into two separate pieces, as described in the Cyber Third Party Risk Program updates earlier. The first part of the document is owned by the legal team, and their updates focused on the legal language, not specific controls. When updating the document, the inclusion of incident notification was of paramount importance. However, they also incorporated language regarding certain ZT principles. This included the requirement for users to adhere to the principle of least privilege and required that vendors meeting the criteria for being systemically critical (a list owned and maintained by TPRM) undertake their own ZT journey. Of course, the wording couldn't be "vendor shall have a ZT journey" for a couple of reasons. First, it would likely result in a definition war over the term *zero trust journey*. Second, it is too nebulous. Instead, the specific principles and controls necessary for achieving ZT were explicitly outlined for vendors in a systemically critical relationship with KC Enterprises.

Monitor and Maintain

The ZT team made an early decision that monitor and maintain would not start at the end of the project, but rather as each row was being completed and the "Scan all content for third-party malicious activity or data theft" was able to begin. Not all the system logs and records would be available on day one and would be available in stages as capabilities were deployed, tested, redesigned, and updated. This meant that the maturity model would evolve as these capabilities were first deployed manually and as time passed they were automated via workflows, APIs, and other connections.

The monitor and maintain incremental enablement aligns with the incremental approach to ZT deployment at KC Enterprises. The initial process of detailing the protect surface and getting an accurate inventory of all third-party users, applications, and infrastructure provided the initial planning and implementation for ZT. However, the design of the architecture and production deployment of a number of automated systems to capture new third-party users, applications, and infrastructure meant that the monitoring process added these new items into the CMDB, SIEM, DLP, and other tools and processes to ensure compliance. Manual processes present during the early stages of ZT third-party deployments were automated based on their risk to the organization.

Similar to the approach the team used to measure systemically critical vendors' adherence in their ZT journey, the decision was made to use the CISA Zero Trust Maturity Model as part of the monitoring and maintenance phase to measure their progress toward becoming a mature program. The goal was to bring all operations into the advanced maturity stage by the end of the first year and to reach the optimal maturity stage by the end of the second year for third-party users, applications, and infrastructure.

Part II: Apply the Lessons from Summary

KC Enterprises is a fictional company, but its situation is far from fictional in terms of what most cyber and third-party practitioners have seen in the last few years. Undeniably, the level of malicious cyber activity has significantly increased since before the COVID pandemic. As a result, the number of potential incidents involving third or fourth parties requiring investigation has also followed this upward trend. Although it is a fictitious company, the intent in covering it is to provide the reader with a way to take the abstract (at times) discussion in the first part of the book into the realm of practical: how would someone do this in reality? The mix of technical, logical, and process changes is complex and will vary from company to company. However, ZT is not a technology or a solution, it is a combination of technical, logical, and process controls to lower the impact when that breach from a third party, or as the result of a third party, does happen.

Acknowledgments

M y first praise is to God, who enabled me to write this book. I also want to acknowledge and thank my technical editor, Jerry Chapman, for helping make this book better and more accurate. Many thanks for the feedback and input from John Kindervag to better refine the zero trust history, strategy, and best practices. Thanks, as well, goes to George Finney for the inspiration on how to connect the dots between third-party risk and zero trust. And finally, I want to thank my Wiley team, Jim Minatel and Kelly Talbot, who are awesome collaborators.

About the Author

Gregory Rasner has worked as a cybersecurity and IT leader in finance, biotech, technology, and software fields. He holds a Bachelor of Arts degree from Claremont McKenna College, along with these certifications: CISSP, CCNA, CIPM, ITIL. Greg is the author of the Third Party Cyber Risk Assessor (TPCRA) training and certification, in collaboration with Third Party Risk Association. He is the author of the book *Cybersecurity and Third-Party Risk: Third Party Threat Hunting* (Wiley, 2021), has written several online articles for major publications, and is a frequent speaker at forums and conferences on related topics. Greg helped create the cybersecurity program at Johnston Community College, is a board member on the Technology Advisory Board, and teaches part-time at JCC as well.

About the Technical Editor

Jerry Wayne Chapman is the Chief Identity Officer (CIdO) at Fischer Identity. With over 25 years of industry experience, Jerry has successfully guided numerous clients in the design and implementation of their enterprise identity and access management (IAM) strategies, in ways that align with both security and business objectives. His job roles have spanned enterprise architecture, solution engineering, and software architecture and development. Jerry is active in the technical working group at the Identity Defined Security Alliance (IDSA), where he was the group's original technical architect. Jerry is a certified Forrester Zero Trust Strategist, is a co-chair of the Cloud Security Alliance (CSA), and is a co-author of the book *Zero Trust Security: An Enterprise Guide* (Apress, 2021). Jerry has a Bachelor of Science degree in computer information systems from DeVry University and is currently pursuing a degree in applied mathematics from Southern New Hampshire University.

Index

213